The Buddha's
MEDICINE FOR THE MIND
Cultivating Wisdom and Compassion

GESHE TASHI TSERING
Chenrezig Institute

The Buddha's
MEDICINE FOR THE MIND
Cultivating Wisdom and Compassion

GESHE TASHI TSERING

Chenrezig Institute

Translated by Lozang Zopa

Acknowledgements

My thanks to everyone who has helped in the production of this book: from the translator to those who work at the centres where these talks were given, to those who work at Lothian Books and beyond. Thank you for all your help.

For information about the Chenrezig Institute visit
   www.chenrezig.com.au

Thomas C. Lothian Pty Ltd
132 Albert Road, South Melbourne, Victoria 3205
www.lothian.com.au

Copyright © Geshe Tashi Tsering and FPMT Australia,
   trading as Chenrezig Institute 2004
Translated and edited by Lozang Zopa for Chenrezig Institute 2004
First published 2004

All rights reserved. No part of this publication may be reproduced, stored in a retrieval system or transmitted in any form by any means without the prior permission of the copyright owner. Enquiries should be made to the publisher.

National Library of Australia
Cataloguing-in-Publication data:

   Tsering, Geshe Tashi.
   The Buddha's medicine for the mind.
   ISBN 0 7344 0565 0

   1. Buddhism — Doctrines. 2. Spiritual life — Buddhism.
   I. Title.

294.3420423

Series Editor: Alison Ribush
Managing Editor: Magnolia Flora
Editors: Alison Ribush and Sue Harvey
Cover design: Viola Ecographic Design
Cover art: David Brooks
Internal design and typesetting: Caz Brown
Printed in Australia by Griffin Press

Contents

PART ONE
The mind

1 **Medicine for the mind**   5
   View and conduct   8
   Buddhism and the West   10

2 **The nature of mind**   15
   The need to understand our minds   17
   The mind   18

3 **Buddha nature**   35
   The relative nature of mind   43
   The ultimate nature of mind   44
   Awakening buddha potential   60

PART TWO
The Three Principal Aspects of the Path

4 **A history of the lam rim and Gelug lineage**   77
   The life of Atisha   79
   The life of Lama Tsongkhapa   83
   The Great Treatise on the Stages of the
      Path to Enlightenment   90
   Beings of the Three Scopes   92
   The Three Principal Aspects of the Path
      by Lama Tsongkhapa   94

5	**Renunciation: the intention to definitively emerge**	99
	Verses 1 to 5 of *The Three Principal Aspects of the Path*	101
	Renunciation	103
	Why we need renunciation	115
6	**Bodhicitta: the mind of enlightenment**	155
	Verses 6 to 8 of *The Three Principal Aspects of the Path*	157
	What is bodhicitta?	159
	Developing a mind drawn to others	160
	Reverse order of generating a mind of enlightenment	162
	What is compassion?	164
	Developing equanimity	166
	Cultivating equanimity through meditation	174
	The sevenfold instruction on cause and effect	181
	Meditating on the two techniques	199
7	**The correct view**	201
	Verses 9 to 14 of *The Three Principal Aspects of the Path*	203
	Why cultivate correct view?	205
	Misapprehending the self and the wisdom that realises selflessness	216
	Two truths	226
	Seclusion	235
8	**Working with the mind**	239
	What is the heart of Buddhism?	241
Glossary		245
Notes		263
Recommended reading		264
Index		265

PART ONE
The mind

The Buddha's teachings are intended to bring greater happiness to this world by encouraging altruistic actions and discouraging harmful ones. Since actions begin in the mind, the purpose of Buddhist thought and practice is to reduce the disturbing emotions that afflict the mind.

In Part One of this book I discuss the mind and how it works — you cannot understand Buddhism deeply without understanding this. Understanding the mind will give you an insight into disturbing emotions, the states of mind that create suffering for ourselves and for others. This is very important, for we must first recognise such states if we are to eliminate them. How can you get rid of something if you do not know what it is? For these reasons, Chapter 2 is on the nature of mind.

Our discussion of the mind's relative and ultimate natures leads us to buddha nature, which is discussed in Chapter 3. Buddhist texts say that 'buddha nature' — the potential to become a buddha — exists in every being, including the smallest insect. But animals cannot analyse things to the same degree as humans. The limits of their intelligence restrict the extent to which they can develop their buddha nature. With greater intelligence and ability to reason, humans are able to develop their buddha nature much more. But while all humans have the potential, not all humans enjoy the circumstances that are conducive to and supportive of its development. Thus it is all the more important for those humans who do enjoy such conditions to make the effort and develop their buddha nature through practice and study.

A person can develop their potential for buddhahood by developing renunciation, the mind of enlightenment, and a correct view. These three are explained in Part Two, in Chapters 5, 6 and 7, which are dedicated to the Three Principal Aspects of the Path. Chapter 4 includes a brief history of the *lam rim*, or Stages of the Path, literature and the life story of Lama Tsongkhapa, the author of *The Three Principal Aspects of the Path*. This gives the reader a taste of the Tibetan setting and instills the confidence that these teachings have a sound source in the tradition.

I have chosen these topics as an introduction to Buddhism with a Western audience in mind.

1

Medicine for the mind

Buddhism is founded upon the view of interdependence and non-harming conduct. The way we understand the world influences the way we act, so view and conduct are closely related to one another. This introductory chapter explains how these two apply to our everyday lives.

The desire for happiness is common to us all. Everyone wants to be happy, but various circumstances prevent this. Why do we encounter frustration and unhappiness instead of the deep and lasting happiness we seek? Could there be a cause, or do happiness and unhappiness just occur randomly?

Unhappiness is like a side-effect of an illness. If the illness is properly diagnosed and treated, the side effects disappear. Recognising this, the Buddha diagnosed the illnesses that lead to unhappiness and prescribed a cure for them. The *Dharma*, the Buddha's teachings, are the Buddha's medicine for the mind.

The Buddha knew from experience that unhappiness is a product of disturbing emotions. These emotions have a negative influence on our state of mind and cause us to act negatively. The Buddha realised that if we could uproot disturbing emotions, we would uproot the causes of unhappiness and plant the seeds for true happiness.

But as we might expect, the remedy for unhappiness does not come as a pill. If we want to achieve total physical health we must follow a complete regimen of eating the right food, exercising and seeing the doctor. Similarly, to achieve a deep and lasting happiness that is free of all suffering, we must have a comprehensive program. We must learn what causes our unhappiness and how to overcome it. We must learn what causes happiness and how to encourage those things. And finally, we must internalise what we learn and apply it in our lives.

View and conduct

There are a wide variety of Buddhist teachings, but basically they constitute a view of how things are and the conduct we are encouraged to adopt in light of this. Essentially, the Buddhist view is that all things are interdependent. This interdependence has many different levels, but put simply it refers to the fact that positive effects are produced in dependence upon positive causes and negative effects are produced in dependence upon negative causes. This is the basic premise of *karma*, or actions and their effects.

We can see interdependence at play in the external world. Without a seed, a plant cannot grow. The seed is the cause of the plant, while the plant and its products are the effects of the seed. Just as poisons come from poisonous plants, poisonous plants come from the seeds of poisonous plants. Thus poisons, poisonous plants and the seeds themselves are interdependent; one relies upon the other. The same is true of medicine and the medicinal plants and seeds it comes from.

The principles of cause and effect, as seen in the external environment, govern our inner life as well. Internally, a positive cause is one that has a positive effect, namely that of pleasure and happiness. A negative cause is one that has a negative effect, namely displeasure and suffering. Since our own actions cause one or the other, the principles of cause and effect offer simple guidelines on how to lead our lives.

By nature, we all want to be happy and we do not want distress. Happiness, being a positive effect, naturally arises from positive causes. Conversely, negative causes naturally foster unhappiness, which is a negative and unpleasant effect. Knowing the difference between positive and negative causes, we can embrace and discard certain behaviours to bring about the happiness we seek and avoid unwanted distress.

According to Buddhism, the most positive cause is to cultivate goodwill towards others. The most negative cause is to have ill will towards others. Since suffering arises as a result of ill will and happiness results from abandoning that, we should abandon ill will. This is what the Buddha encouraged his students to do. Thus it is clear how the type of conduct encouraged in Buddhism is based on the interdependent nature of things.

Ill will towards others naturally stops when we begin to cultivate goodwill for others. As a result, we enjoy the fruits of altruism and avoid the suffering that results from malice. This is why the Buddhist texts say the main practice of Buddhism is to refrain from harming others. Buddhist practice begins with giving up ill will.

Buddhism and the West

When a person, Westerner or otherwise, abandons ill will towards others, their life becomes meaningful. A meaningful life brings benefit to both oneself and others. There are many people who have, through their interest in and practice of the Buddhist teachings, made their lives meaningful. In the process of doing so, they refrain from taking life, stealing, engaging in sexual misconduct, speaking harshly and so on. These behaviours are avoided because they are harmful to others. Buddhist practice is based upon a conscious rejection of these types of acts.

I believe the Buddhist teachings can help Westerners lead more meaningful lives. As children, you are sent to school to get an education — an education that is, for the most part, unparalleled in other parts of the world. This tradition of education has fostered an academic and scientific tradition, which in turn has led to many significant and impressive achievements. Westerners have made discoveries and advancements seen nowhere else in the world. You have a sound foundation of knowledge and training to build upon. That foundation can be augmented by Buddhist teachings on actions and their effects.

There are some things about Buddhism you will learn through examples and analogies. Other things can only be understood in the light of your own experience. In comparing the teachings to your own experience you will appreciate how we all bear responsibility for our own actions and how our own actions impact upon others. And with a greater understanding of personal responsibility comes the opportunity for greater happiness, not just for ourself but for others as well.

This is the type of thinking taught in the Mahayana, or 'Great Vehicle'. The Mahayana is one of the main branches of the Buddhist tradition and its teachings are central to Tibetan Buddhism. The Mahayana teachings stress the importance of cultivating goodwill towards others, not just giving up ill will towards them. Cultivating this goodwill involves developing the perfect intention to help others.

We must overcome our indifference to the plight of others if we are to develop the perfect intention to help others. Being indifferent to the welfare of others is self-cherishing. Indifference contributes strongly to ill will and for that reason we must remedy it and increase the degree to which we cherish others. It is important to cherish the well-being of all others, be they friend, foe or stranger, and not just the people we are close to.

The benefits of overcoming ill will and cultivating goodwill for all are twofold. Firstly, if we cherish the well-being of all others, we will refrain from harmful actions, such as killing, stealing and so forth. Secondly, the seeds — the potencies of mind — left behind by such acts in the past will be robbed of their power to produce suffering. Disturbing emotions pollute and dirty the mind; they create unhappiness in this life and lead us to act negatively in future lives. Loving-kindness and compassion, on the other hand, have a tremendous capacity to cleanse the mind of such disturbing emotions, and hence they are highly valued. If, with a strong interest in the welfare of others, we make loving-kindness and compassion the core of our practice, this will act as a great wave that cleanses the mind.

With all the advancements of the modern age, we have become so used to convenience that we want everything to be straightforward and simple. If it is not easy to use, forget it! The love of convenience influences many aspects of our life, including our approach to Buddhism. Many of us may feel overwhelmed in the face of such a vast and unfamiliar tradition of philosophy and meditation. The scope and depth of the Buddhist teachings make us think, 'There is so much to do, so much to think about. Even the most basic code of Buddhist ethics involves giving up ten types of actions! How could I do all that?' The Buddha's teachings on appropriate behaviour may seem complicated, but there is no need to be put off. We don't need to be scholars to apply the Buddha's teachings, since pure ethics flow naturally from genuine loving-kindness and compassion.

Why would someone who sincerely wishes for the happiness of others do something to harm them? They wouldn't. The heartfelt wish that others be happy and free of suffering naturally quells the wish to kill, steal and commit other harmful actions. This is why the Buddhist teachings, especially loving-kindness and compassion, are so relevant to those of us who love convenience and simplicity. Loving-kindness and compassion are like a labour-saving device, a lawnmower that cuts through the dense grass of Buddhist techniques to reveal their innermost essence. In a hectic life with little time for advanced study, you can still find relief in the simple method of developing goodwill for others.

Buddhism in modern times

These days, we have powerful machines that can clean the external world. Loving-kindness, compassion and a greater concern for the well-being of others are powerful machines that cleanse the internal world of the mind and activate its positive potential. While advanced external technology has only become available in recent decades, the Buddha devised such advanced internal technology hundreds and hundreds of years ago.

This analogy may seem flippant, but I do believe that Buddhism is compatible with Western attitudes. Westerners like to understand things clearly, beyond a shadow of a doubt. Buddhism uses logic and reasoning to eliminate doubts and distinguish between what is faulty and what is good. In fact, Buddhism puts a high priority on developing wisdom. In this respect it embraces one of the central concerns of the modern age in general, and Westerners in particular: the desire to know things clearly without a doubt. If a person practises properly, he or she can develop wisdom. Furthermore, the knowledge we possess today far surpasses that which we had in the past. But the way we wield this knowledge is controlled by attachment and hostility. Holding to the inherent superiority of one's own position while seeking to overcome that of others, we use our knowledge to accomplish great acts that quite often cause great harm. Though this may not be our intention, our sometimes clumsy use of knowledge often causes damage.

If people in these modern times could apply the techniques for developing loving-kindness and compassion that the Buddha taught over two thousand years ago, we could use our vast store of knowledge to bring about a pure and stable peace in this world. In fact, I believe that such an outcome is certain if we can bridge these two bodies of knowledge, science and Buddhism. When knowledge lacks the support of compassion and loving-kindness, it benefits some while harming others. The best approach is the one the Buddha advised: to cherish all impartially and to extend our sense of care and concern to everyone. Thus I believe that Buddhism is not only helpful to Westerners, but also quite amenable to modern times as well.

2

The nature of mind

Mind creates and shapes our experience. The mind is not fixed and intractable; it is pliant and receptive. Working with the mind we can remove ingrained attitudes that create suffering for ourselves and others. We can cultivate altruistic and unmistaken states of mind that lead to happiness for ourselves and others. We study the mind to understand it, for when we understand the mind we understand what disturbs and what nourishes the mind. A person who has mastered his or her own mind is a light unto themself. Such a person understands that the key to happiness lies within us and nowhere else, and that the path to freedom lies in conquering the real enemies, disturbing emotions.

The teachings in this chapter are based on Phurbu Chog's study of awareness and knowledge entitled *An Explanation of Subject and Object*.[1]

> *You will not find explanations of a creator god in Buddhist texts. If a Buddhist were asked about a 'creator of the world', they would respond by saying it is the mind. The mind is the creator of the world and a mind free of mistaken perception will protect us from suffering.*

The need to understand our minds

In all things, an altruistic motivation is very important, but altruism alone will not alleviate the suffering of another person. Buddhahood is not attained through prayer alone; we must also accumulate the causes for it. To become a buddha we must apply the teachings in our lives so that our thoughts, words and actions are in harmony with our altruistic motivation. To do that effectively, we need to understand the mind and how it works. What we learn will help us to help others.

Don't be discouraged if you do not immediately understand everything you read in this book. By nature, we like to perform well, so we get upset when we do not understand. But this is just a sign of the pride we are born with. Pride creates certain hopes and expectations. We do not have to be upset when we do not live up to them. If our pride is hurt and we get upset, we are likely to become angry or envious. We study the mind and the teachings in the hope that we will be happier as a result. If instead our efforts bring pride, envy and anger that in turn lead to unhappiness, we have turned what can be good into something bad. Relax and try as hard as you can to absorb this material — don't worry, be happy.

Studying mind and the way it works can be very valuable. The development of mind depends on the development of particular states of mind, so we must understand the way the mind is influenced by them. We must understand the difference between wholesome, helpful states of mind and unwholesome, harmful states. Certain states of mind, such as loving-kindness and compassion, ought to be adopted, while others like anger and envy ought to be discarded. Our minds will improve and develop if we employ this knowledge; in short, we will be happier.

The mind

A Tibetan master, Kachen Yeshe Gyaltshan (1713–93), observed that intelligent people are not content to merely subsist; rather, their thoughts turn to the bigger picture. Intelligent people think about the meaning of life and what comes afterwards, asking themselves, 'Why are we so powerless over our existence?' On reflection, it is clear that there are causes for our circumstances being the way they are, and that these causes are not dissimilar to our experiences.

Effects do not arise without a cause. Effects arise from causes that are similar or compatible to them in type. Happiness and unhappiness are no exception; it is a mistake to believe otherwise. Misunderstanding this natural principle creates even more unhappiness.

According to the protector Nagarjuna, ignorance lies at the root of the causal chain that places us in a cycle of suffering.[2] We do not understand the nature of self; we instinctively misapprehend the self, acting as if it existed from its own side. It seems to us as if the self or 'I' somehow stands alone, an entity independent of body and mind. But how could 'I' exist independently of body and mind? The self depends upon body and mind, but it appears to be independent of body and mind. Yet this is a false appearance created by ignorance. There is no self that is independent of body and mind; such a self does not exist.

We operate under the assumption that 'I' am as 'I' seem to be. Instinctively, we assume that others do too. We cling to this 'I' so that when threatened, the strong sense that '*He* is trying to harm *me*' makes us become angry; or when someone else helps us the sense that '*She* is helping *me*', leads to attachment.

Disturbing emotions like anger, attachment, envy and pride are based on and inflamed by our ignorance of self. Since we do not understand how the self actually exists, we cling to the appearances that our misapprehensions of self create and fall prey to disturbing emotions. Under their influence we perform actions that cause us to be reborn in cyclic existence. In short, actions and disturbing emotions underpin cyclic existence.

We must recognise how we misapprehend the self if we are to understand the way it actually exists. In doing so, we will see that there is a discrepancy between the way the self appears to be and the way it actually exists. The self appears to exist in and of itself, but it does not. To understand the nature of self we must understand how the self is empty of independent existence, which is its 'emptiness'. This is explained in more detail in Chapter 7.

The actions of body, speech and mind motivated by disturbing emotions perpetuate cyclic existence, or what is known as *samsara*. Such actions place seeds and imprints in our mind in the form of potentials or potencies, which later ripen into pleasant or unpleasant experiences. Once these seeds have been activated they come to fruition and create the circumstances of our lives. Misapprehending the self conditions our mind so that every thought and action bolsters cyclic existence. Aryadeva (second to third century CE) said that consciousness is the seed of conditioned existence since the karmic seeds and imprints that perpetuate it are left on the mind. Without mind, we would not cycle within cyclic existence, because without a mind there would be no place for karmic seeds and imprints to be stored.

Disturbing emotions are the real enemies. They are the roots of cyclic existence. But that is only one part of the equation. There are in fact many other necessary elements, like mind, actions, seeds and imprints. Disturbing emotions alone cannot do very much unless they are acted upon. If disturbing emotions are not expressed in physical or verbal actions, their full fruits will not follow.

Many respected Buddhist masters such as Chandrakirti (540–600 CE) and Vasubandhu (400–480 CE) agreed that the mind, in conjunction with actions, establishes not only the animate and inanimate world, but also the experiences therein. Mind determines the circumstances of our existence, whether we continue within cyclic existence or pass beyond all sorrow.

Healing the mind

Medical doctors study anatomy and physiology in-depth because a great deal of knowledge is required to properly treat the disorders and diseases of the body. For a physician, a thorough understanding of the basis for illness — the body

— is indispensable. In order to be an effective physician, a person must also study medicine and the techniques for treating disease.

The Buddha is often compared to a doctor. His teachings are like medicine, while the supportive spiritual community are like nurses. The patient in this case is the mind. The disease is that of the disturbing emotions. Our goal is to heal the mind of disturbing emotions by applying medicinal teachings. For this to be effective, we must know what is afflicted. We must understand the basis for the sickness of unhappiness — the mind.

It is said that 'the disease of anger is cured by the medicine of loving-kindness', so you might say that we are engaged in a form of medical training. What does anger harm? Anger harms the mind because mind experiences the suffering that ensues from anger. Loving-kindness can heal the wounds caused by anger, but to fully understand the healing potential of loving-kindness we must know the mind.

Just as a good doctor must be well versed in the body, the illnesses that beset it, and the medicine used to treat it, we must be well versed in the mind that receives treatment, the disturbing emotions that afflict it, and the medicinal remedies. Knowledge of these three elements enables us to offer medicinal remedies to others in their time of need. We can also apply this knowledge in our own lives when we fall prey to disturbing emotions. In this way our study of mind will benefit both ourself and others.

If we recognise mind, disturbing emotions and their remedies, we will be happy and pleasantly disposed at all times, whether we are alone in retreat or in the midst of a bustling crowd. We will be happy even when surrounded by a group of people behaving terribly because we will have on hand the antidote that dispels disturbing emotions.

I strongly believe that many mental and emotional difficulties stem from a lack of study and training of the mind. If we do not train and study the mind, we will not know how to deal with problems when they occur. Without the proper tools and training, we cannot skilfully deal with our problems. We may end up exacerbating the situation as a result.

Many people attribute their present unhappiness to events that occurred in their childhood, but there is nothing we can do to change the past. There is often no reason to repeatedly dredge up the past, especially when it disturbs us. It is much better to spend our time learning about how to address and deal with mental and emotional difficulties.

Mental states

We have both mind and mental events. Mental events are also called states of mind or mental factors. Mental events are of two types: they are positive or negative. Yet positive or negative, they are all adventitious, only temporary. They come and they go, whereas the mind is continuously present. Mind cannot be seen with the eyes. The mind is intangible and immaterial.

All sentient beings have a mind and this mind is clear and knowing. The mind is an entity that has the capacity to know things clearly. Buddha Shakyamuni said, 'The nature of the mind is luminous.' This statement can be explained in a few ways. On the one hand, it means that nothing stains the nature of mind. On the other hand it means that the mind does not inherently exist.

The nature of mind has two aspects: a relative aspect and an ultimate aspect. We will mention these again when we discuss buddha potential in Chapter 3. To really understand our potential for buddhahood we must understand the nature of mind.

We also have to understand the way mind works. The mind is not free to engage with objects of its own accord. The mind engages objects with the assistance of different mental events. These mental events arise to accompany mind and in the process mind begins to resemble them.

The mind is always accompanied by five specific mental events: feeling, discrimination, intention, contact and attention. These are known as the five omnipresent mental events. Mind cannot engage objects without them. It would be impossible to have a mind without these five mental events.

Why is feeling important? Feelings are pleasant, unpleasant or neutral. If there were no feelings, the mind could not experience things as pleasant, unpleasant or neutral.

Why is discrimination important? If there was no discrimination the mind could not distinguish between one thing and another. Discrimination helps the mind note and mark the differences between this and that.

Why is intention important? Intention is mental volition. Without intention we could not act or accumulate karma. Intention initiates actions of all types. Intention is linked to the aggregate of formation and karma.

Why is contact important? If there were no contact, mind could not engage objects. Mind must come into contact with an object before it can do anything further with it. Such contact involves a mind, a sense faculty and an object.

Why is attention important? Attention is required for meditation. Attention directs the mind towards particular objects, allowing us to remain for long periods of time on a specific one.

These five mental events support the mind's experience of objects. Intention directs mind towards an object. Contact brings mind into contact with it. Feeling arises, instilling pleasure, displeasure or neutrality in the mind. Discrimination sorts out the object's different elements. Attention helps the mind focus on any given one.

The feelings we experience relate to the distinctions that discrimination makes. The karma we accumulate depends on the intention that drives the mind, the way we contact objects and the amount of attention we pay to that. Mental events give direction to the mind. The mind does not move autonomously towards positive or negative actions. It is steered in either a positive or negative direction by the mental events that accompany it.

Mind and mental events perform different functions. Mind sees the object while these events or states of mind see its particular features. Mind may focus on a particular object but does not engage its individual aspects; those are engaged by individual states of mind. In other words, mind simply observes; individual states of mind analyse and ascertain.

The mind and the mental events that occur within it are a single entity. The five omnipresent states are essentially identical with mind, distinguished from mind only by conceptual analysis. To speak of mind is to speak about the basic awareness of an object, without isolating any specific difference or function. To speak of states of mind is to speak about individual functions of our basic awareness.

If any of the five omnipresent events are missing, our experience of an object will not be complete. Without feeling, the object would not be experienced as pleasant or unpleasant. Without discrimination, the unique features of

The nature of mind

an object would not be apprehended. Without intention, the mind would not be directed towards the object. Without attention, the mind would not focus on a specific thing. Without contacting the object, there would be no basis for feelings and so forth. For these reasons, the full experience of an object requires that all five mental events be present.

Mind comes to resemble the events that accompany it; if the states of mind are disturbed, mind is also disturbed. If a displeased state of mind arises, the mind becomes displeased. Anger is a disturbed state of mind; it arises within mind and colours the mind in a distinctive way but is not the mind. The presence of just one disturbed state of mind disturbs both the mind itself and any other states of mind manifest at that moment.

Cultivating positive states of mind has the opposite effect. Take loving-kindness for instance. Loving-kindness involves empathy for others. Feeling drawn to others, we wish for them to be happy. As we do so, the mind itself becomes empathetic and assumes the aspect of loving-kindness. Just as anger upsets the mind and gives it an angry aspect, loving-kindness brings peace of mind and a caring aspect.

The mind is impermanent. It is produced in dependence upon causes and conditions so it is in a constant state of flux, changing from moment to moment. The mind will naturally change from moment to moment, but if we want it to change in specific ways we must actively work with it. To change the way we think, we must harness discrimination and the other mental events. The momentary changes linked to the impermanent nature of the mind are not the same as the conscious changes that rely on positive mental events. In particular, these conscious changes rely upon discrimination. Sometimes our discrimination is accurate, but other times it might err. It is perhaps the busiest, and in some ways most problematic, mental event we have.

The importance of correct discrimination

Discrimination and intention are particularly influential mental events; quite strange things occur when our discrimination goes awry. When I was living in south India, we planted fields of corn around our newly established monastery to support the monks. While the shoots were still small, we had to watch over the fields so elephants would not trample them. Every night a group of five or six monks was sent out with torches to keep elephants out of the paddock. One night when I was out there, we saw an elephant in the distance. My companions said, 'Can you see that? There's an elephant out there!' Though the monks had torches, they were afraid to approach it. While we were standing there watching, it started to move. My companions said, 'Did you see it move? I think it's moving!' Everyone got scared and ran away thinking, 'Oh no! The elephant is moving!' The next day after daybreak we went back to the same spot and the 'elephant' turned out to be a big tree! A tree with big branches blowing in the breeze, but a tree firmly rooted in the ground. And to think we saw an immobile object moving!

In this case, our mistake caused no real harm, but other mistakes can cause problems and suffering. When our discrimination errs, our mind errs as well, leading to all sorts of problems. But how does discrimination work?

In *The Compendium of Knowledge*, the noble Asanga says that discrimination by nature apprehends either a mark or an idea.[3] Perceptual consciousnesses, like eyesight, apprehend 'marks' while conceptual consciousnesses apprehend 'ideas'.

To apprehend a mark means to apprehend the unique aspects of an object that appears to a non-conceptual consciousness. The five senses, which are non-conceptual, apprehend such unique marks — 'unique' in that each type of perception only apprehends a certain type of object and no other. The eye sees shape and colour, the ear hears sound, the nose smells odours, the tongue tastes flavours and so forth. Though discrimination in these cases is non-conceptual, conceptual discrimination often accompanies or ensues from it.

For instance, you may be partial to the colour blue. For you, the sight of blue leads to the conceptual discrimination, 'This is good.' A non-conceptual consciousness acts as the basis for a conceptual consciousness. The conscious identification of a particular hue — 'This is blue' or 'This is red' — depends on a non-conceptual consciousness such as eyesight.

The same principle operates with our sense of smell. Having smelled a particular scent, the nose consciousness may be able to discriminate that scent from others. That discrimination acts as the basis for the thought, 'This is the scent of a rose.' So in practice, non-conceptual and conceptual consciousnesses often arise together.

To apprehend an idea means to apprehend an idea that appears to a conceptual consciousness. Conceptual discriminations do not necessarily rely on the senses. Some arise not in relation to sensory data, but to our way of thinking or our attitudes. For instance, we may mull over a situation and think, 'This is no good. I am not satisfied. This is not enjoyable.' These thoughts do not necessarily correspond to what we take in through our senses; they are more related to thoughts.

Mental illnesses are directly related to errors in our discrimination and disturbances in our state of mind. When a person's ability to discriminate has gone awry, it is very difficult to treat their mental illness solely through external means. Rather than believe everything we perceive, we should investigate things thoroughly before coming to a conclusion, to ensure that our discrimination has not erred.

When a person sits around all day with nothing to do, their mind will entertain any and all manner of thoughts and ideas. These thoughts are not always healthy or productive and can lead to mental and emotional difficulties. In more extreme cases, they may even lead to mental illness. We are better off using our time constructively, in studying or working.

If the person is interested in meditation, he or she ought to try to meditate correctly, not blankly or aimlessly. When we meditate we try to familiarise ourselves with positive states of mind, or analyse and dwell on specific points like emptiness. In sitting with a vacant mind we are doing neither. Correct meditations focus on an object or series of objects without distraction. The whole point of meditation is to stop ourselves from falling under the sway of misconceptions and misguided thoughts. This helps us to use our time wisely and protect ourselves from the negative influence of misconceptions. If we can resist the power of misguided thoughts, incorrect meditation techniques and misconceptions, we will not encounter any great difficulties. There is nothing to worry about.

Karma and intention

Intention is the most important of all mental events because it gives direction to the mind, determining whether we engage with virtuous, non-virtuous, or neutral objects. Just as iron is powerlessly drawn to a magnet, our minds are powerlessly drawn to the object of our intentions.

An intention is a mental action; it may be expressed through either physical or verbal actions. Thus action, or karma, is of two types: the action of intention and the intended action. The action of intention is the thought or impulse to engage in a physical or verbal act. The intended action is the physical or verbal expression of our intention. Karma actually refers to the action of intention but in general usage it includes the intended action and the seeds that are left in the mind as a result.

How do we accumulate karmic seeds? Every physical and verbal action is preceded by mental activity. Goodwill motivates a kind gesture; ill will motivates nasty words. Ill will is the intention to cause mental, emotional or physical harm. Thus, before and during a bad action, ill will is present in our mind. The presence of ill will before and during this act has an impact and influence on the mind due to which a certain potential is left behind. This potential is a karmic seed, a seed planted in our mind by physical, verbal or mental action. The strength or depth of this seed is determined by a number of factors, including how strong our intention is, whether we clearly understand what we are doing, whether we act on our intention and whether the physical and verbal act is completed.

Seeds will remain in the mind until they ripen or are destroyed. Seeds left by negative mental events and actions can be destroyed by the four opponent or antidotal powers. The most important of these four powers are regret for the negative act and a firm resolve not to act that way again in the future. Seeds left by positive mental events and actions can be destroyed by anger.

Even if we do not act on a negative intention, a karmic seed of diminished potency is still left in the mind. This incomplete seed is easier to remove. If it is not destroyed, a negative seed will eventually produce an unpleasant and negative effect while a positive seed will produce a pleasant and positive effect. Karmic seeds do not go to waste even after one hundred aeons. They will come to fruition when the time comes and the conditions assemble.

Actions motivated by the wish to attain buddhahood for the benefit of all sentient beings and dedicated to that end have a special feature. The positive effects of such an act will be experienced many times over without being exhausted. For this reason, virtue dedicated to complete enlightenment is likened to a magnificent tree that bears fruit every season without fail. Such virtues will bear fruit until buddhahood is attained.

A valid realisation or even an excellent and correct understanding of emptiness can prevent virtues from being destroyed by anger. A virtue will not be destroyed by anger if, in dedicating it, we understand that the dedicator, the act of dedication, the virtue that is dedicated and what we are dedicating it to, all lack inherent existence.

Meditation is important but so is applying what we meditate on. If we act on our intention to help others, we place deeper and more stable seeds in our minds. If the seed left by a negative thought is stronger and more grave when acted upon, then the same must be true for positive thoughts! In other words, the states of mind we cultivate should be applied in body and speech to bring maximum benefit.

3

Buddha nature

Buddha nature or buddha potential is the innate potential every being has to become a buddha. Buddha potential has two aspects: the naturally present potential for buddhahood and the potential for buddhahood that needs to be developed. The naturally present potential allows for the transformation from deluded mind to enlightened mind. The potential that needs to be developed is the very mind that undergoes that transformation. However, such a change does not occur spontaneously: it involves hard work and effort, but the results we gain from this effort are the unfathomable qualities of ultimate wisdom, compassion and capacity.

The teachings in this chapter are based on Maitreya's *Sublime Continuum*, a scripture treasured by all Tibetan Buddhists.[1]

> *We hear that all sentient beings have buddha potential, but still we may wonder, 'Is it even possible to attain buddhahood? Can a polluted stream be cleaned?' Just so with our mind and what stains it. Disturbing emotions are neither intrinsic to nor inseparable from mind. They come and they go, like the debris that pollutes a stream. Once they are removed we perceive reality and things in all their diversity, just like a buddha.*

All creatures possess a life-force and a mind. These distinguish sentient beings from non-sentient things. All sentient beings belong to the family of buddhas; that is, they have the potential to attain buddhahood, which is what 'buddha potential' means. For a thing to become a buddha it must have a mind, so clearly it is important to understand the mind, its nature and its functions.

We can all agree that body and mind exist because we all have certain physical and mental difficulties. Our common experience helps us accept the existence of 'mind'. Mind is neither wholesome nor unwholesome by its nature; rather, it is neutral and malleable. Mind can be steered in either direction, and which path it takes depends on the various mental events that manifest, be they positive or negative.

As for buddha nature, first we must understand 'buddha' and then we can begin to consider whether we possess the nature of a buddha. A buddha is a being who has developed the qualities of wisdom, compassion and ability, to their utmost extent. Since these qualities naturally exist within us, each and every one of us can become a 'buddha'.

A buddha has fully realised wisdom; such consummate or ultimate wisdom knows everything without exception. A person who has developed ultimate wisdom knows even hidden and subtle matters. Such a person would know what another person has concealed in the palm of their hand. They would understand even very subtle things, for if they didn't, they would be ignorant of at least one thing and not have consummate wisdom.

A buddha has fully developed compassion; consummate or ultimate compassion requires equal concern for all beings without exception, regardless of whether they help or harm you. Someone who has developed consummate compassion is concerned with the well-being of all others. A buddha doesn't reserve compassion only for those they like.

Consummate or ultimate ability is the ability to alleviate

another's suffering in whichever way is required. Should we develop ability to its utmost extent, from our own side, we could benefit millions of others according to their disposition, temperament and character. Though this 'ability' is quite difficult to account for, someone who possesses it can alleviate the discomfort of others, regardless of its degree or subtlety.

Anyone who develops wisdom and compassion to their utmost extent will not only be able to benefit others, but will also be able to benefit themselves as well. In fact, the power behind consummate ability is derived from wisdom and compassion themselves. Developing consummate wisdom involves discarding undesirable states of mind and coming to know all things. In order to develop compassion to its utmost extent a person must cultivate the desire to do something about the suffering one sees, so ability is not separate from the other two qualities.

What is the difference between a buddha's mind and our minds? By nature, they are the same. However, our minds are obscured by adventitious stains, whereas a buddha's mind is not. For instance, the water of a stream might be clean and pure by nature, but because of the terrain it passes through it may become murky. If we filter the water, we can remove the silt and debris clouding it and it will be clean and pure once again.

So due to temporary conditions or circumstances, a stream may be dirty and its water unfit for use. Though we may not see it, the water itself is by nature pure: it can be filtered and cleaned and used for drinking, cooking and washing. This is just like our minds: they are by nature pure, and we can cleanse the temporary obscuring defilements from them. The stains or defilements of mind are disturbing emotions and what they leave behind. To say they are 'adventitious' means they are surface stains that can be removed. They do not permeate the nature of mind.

There are five main disturbing emotions: desirous attachment, anger, pride, envy and ignorance. When any of these arise, the mind begins to resemble them so that they seem to infect the very essence of mind. Like the grime in soiled clothing or the impurities in turbid water, disturbing emotions appear to be indivisible and non-distinct from the mind; but they do not permeate the nature of mind and thus can be removed.

How can we cleanse the mind of disturbing emotions? How do defilements arise in the first place? Defiling disturbing emotions arise in response to erroneous perceptions and conceptions: errors that occur when we apprehend an object in an incorrect way. One way to combat disturbing emotions is to cultivate a state of mind that is the opposite of the disturbing emotion itself. For instance, strong loving-kindness can overpower anger. The longer loving-kindness remains, the more anger is dispelled.

Yet this method does not eliminate anger altogether. To completely uproot anger and its seeds we must overturn the foundation it rests upon, the misapprehension of self. The misapprehension of self does not accurately perceive the self; it holds the self to exist from its own side, independent of body and mind. Just as loving-kindness is the opposite of anger, the wisdom that realises selflessness is the opposite of the misapprehension of self. The way this wisdom sees the self is contrary to the way the misapprehension sees the self. In developing this wisdom we understand how the misapprehension is incorrect and replace it with a new, correct way of viewing the self. A wisdom that realises selflessness is the only thing that can directly counter the misapprehension of self. When wisdom stops misapprehension, it cleanses the root of the disturbing emotions. All disturbing emotions will permanently cease once their root is destroyed.

This illustrates a basic Buddhist principle: a valid awareness will act as an antidote to the wrong awareness opposite to it. Disturbing emotions are both based on a wrong awareness — the misapprehension of self — and are themselves wrong awarenesses. Anger, for instance, is wrong in that it exaggerates a person or thing's unappealing aspects. Desirous attachment is wrong in that it exaggerates a person or thing's appealing aspects. We can stop disturbing emotions from becoming manifest by developing a relevant, valid awareness, like loving-kindness for anger, or we can destroy their foundation — the misapprehension of self — by developing the wisdom that realises selflessness.

When we have loving-kindness for someone, anger does not get the opportunities it needs to arise. But anger may arise later once that loving-kindness fades, so it only temporarily stops anger. To completely stop anger and eliminate the seeds of anger we must destroy the misapprehensions of self that support it. Both of these methods are effective in their own way, the one temporarily stopping the opportunities where disturbing emotions can arise, and the other destroying even the seeds that produce disturbing emotions for all time.

Where is the potential for buddhahood? It lies in the nature of our minds. Thus it is extremely important that we see the nature of mind as it is. Everyone would agree that we have both a body and mind. Of course, the term 'mind' is viewed with some hesitancy in scientific circles. Since it cannot be seen, many scientists have difficulty defining 'mind'. But no one denies that we are conscious, cognising beings. Even a scientist sceptical of the term 'mind' does not refute our ability to know.

The sperm of the father and ovum of the mother are

the substantial causes for our body. At a certain point, these causes are exhausted and can no longer sustain the body, so we die and take rebirth, assuming another body. Mind on the other hand is not tossed away like the body. Rather, mind exists in a continuity throughout successive lives, for the substantial cause of mind must come from a previous moment of a similar type. The substantial cause cannot be found within the elements arising from the sperm and ovum.

Once again, where does buddha potential lie? It lies in the essence or nature of mind [Tib. *sems kyi ngo bo*]. 'What is the nature of mind?' you may ask. The mind has both a relative and ultimate nature, like two sides of a coin. Mind is not actually divided, but speaking of it in this way helps us to understand buddha nature more clearly.

The relative nature of mind

Like all phenomena, the nature of mind has both a relative mode of being and an ultimate mode. The mind is by nature an illuminating and knowing entity. In other words, the mind's relative mode of being is as a clear and knowing entity. In Tibetan this phrase leaves room for interpretation: 'clear' can be read as either an adverb or an adjective, so 'clear and knowing' can mean that mind is an entity with the capacity to clearly know objects. Alternatively, it can mean that mind is clear. That is, mind is intangible yet illuminating; immaterial but aware and cognisant of things. I tend to emphasise the latter interpretation.

That mind has the capacity to know objects is beyond dispute. But what are the limits? Mind's capacity for knowledge and awareness is unlimited. In other words, Buddhists believe in the limitless potential of mind, which is similar to the scientific presentation of the brain. I have heard scientists claim that ordinary humans only use a fraction of the brain's capacity — just the tip of the iceberg, so to speak. Scientists say that if we could overcome our inability to harness more of the brain's capacity, we could not even measure its full potential. Whether or not we use the same names and terms as scientists, the implications are the same.

As all beings have a mind, all beings have buddha potential, regardless of whether it has been awakened or cultivated. Buddhist texts say, 'All beings are fit to attain buddhahood at some point.'

The ultimate nature of mind

The Buddhist assertion that all beings are fit to attain buddhahood is based on the fact that we all possess mind and therefore the emptiness of mind. When a person attains buddhahood, he or she attains four 'buddha bodies', the two dharma bodies and the two form bodies. At that point the person's mind becomes the wisdom dharma body and the emptiness of mind becomes the essential dharma body. Since mind and the emptiness of mind are fit to become the dharma bodies of a buddha, anyone with a mind is fit to become a buddha. But how does this transformation happen?

In the sutras, Buddha Shakyamuni taught two points showing that the mind and its emptiness are fit to become dharma bodies, or *dharmakayas*. The first of these two points is that the nature of mind is luminous clear light; the second is that stains are adventitious or temporary. In his *Sublime Continuum*, Maitreya says, 'Like a jewel, space and pure water, the nature of mind is ever undefiled.'[2] This illustrates how the nature of mind is luminous clear light.

The jewel is an analogy for natural purity, a precious substance pure by nature. Even if certain impurities may cling to it, those impurities are alien to its nature and can be removed.

Just as in the English language 'space' can mean 'outer space', 'sky' and the space between two objects, the Tibetan word for 'space' has multiple meanings. Colloquially it means 'outer space' and 'sky'. Technically, 'space' is a negation that does not imply anything else; it is simply 'the absence of any tangible obstruction'. The analogy refers to its colloquial meaning of 'sky'. The sky is by nature free of clouds, though from time to time clouds may obscure it. Similarly, water is by nature clean, even though various debris and pollutants may accrue as it passes down a watercourse.

The luminous nature of mind is like gold free of impurities, the sky free of clouds and water free of pollutants. Though 'luminous' also describes the mind's relative nature, when discussing buddha potential, the emphasis is on the mind's ultimate nature, its emptiness. We can speak about the emptiness of mind, but it is most important that we are introduced to it so that we actually understand it.

One significant difference between the Buddhist understanding of 'mind' and the predominant scientific one is that Buddhists say 'mind' is immaterial, that is, not made of matter. According to Buddhists, 'mind' is an intangible illuminating entity, whereas many scientists would say that 'mind' is reducible to brain functions. According to the scientific position, 'mind' would be no more than brain matter.

In its relative nature the mind itself is clear and cognising and has the potential to know any and every thing. Yet mind does not exist from its own side. Mind has not a shred of inherent existence. This emptiness is mind's ultimate nature.

In Buddhist texts, buddha nature is said to have two aspects, 'the naturally present potential' and 'the potential that needs to be developed'. The mind's lack of inherent or true existence is 'the naturally present potential', while the mind itself is 'the potential that needs to be developed'. The mind itself is an aware entity that is constantly present.

It is accompanied by various mental events, or states of mind, such as wisdom and compassion. Like all mental events, wisdom and compassion are temporary: they come and go while mind remains. Wisdom and compassion are positive mental events. Pride, envy, attachment and so on are negative mental events that conflict with them.

Positive mental events such as wisdom and compassion can be developed because they are adventitious and arise in dependence upon conditions. Since the mind begins to resemble the states that accompany it, developing positive states of mind allows us to develop the mind itself. With time, we can increase the positive qualities of wisdom and compassion while abandoning negative mental states. Eventually, as negative mental states are completely abandoned and positive ones reach their fullest expression, mind also reaches its fullest expression and we become buddhas. This is how we develop 'the potential that needs to be developed'. As the ultimate nature of mind is inextricably linked with the mind that undergoes changes, the mind's ultimate nature reaches the state of buddhahood together with mind. This is how we develop 'the naturally present potential'.

We must understand the way mind works to fully understand how to control our states of mind. When we want a cup of tea or a bite to eat, we develop the aspiration or intention to drink or eat. This aspiration occurs in conjunction with mind; since the aspiration is present in mind, the mind thinks of food and drink. The mind does not engage in things and events freely; it does so through the influence of different mental events. If mind were free, static and unaffected by mental events, it would be very difficult to work with and improve. Fortunately, mental events give direction to the mind so it is possible to work with mind. By controlling which mental events arise we can control the mind.

The more we cultivate positive states of mind and are able to sustain them, the better the mind becomes. Alternatively, the more common and lasting negative states of mind are, the more negative the mind becomes. States of mind steer the mind, so we need to exert influence on which states arise.

Though there are many different mental events, basically they are either positive or negative, while some are neutral. Wisdom and compassion are limitless, as is the mind's capacity for clarity and knowing. The limitless potential of mind can be developed by focusing on limitless positive states of mind. This is how we work with the mind itself to develop and actualise its potential.

What about the ultimate nature of mind? Mind does not exist from its own side. Mind does not inherently exist. Mind does not truly exist. What does this mean? It means that mind is merely imputed or labelled onto a basis. The mind does not exist independently of all other things. Though it might seem to be an autonomous, stand-alone entity, it is not. The mind's lack of inherent existence is the 'emptiness' of mind.

Developing the wish to be free of suffering, or, more literally, the intention to definitively emerge; cultivating loving-kindness and compassion; understanding the ultimate nature of things and events; these provide us with the necessary structure for developing the mind. Such things can be cultivated in meditation. To meditate means to bring something to mind and familiarise or acquaint ourselves with it. Having developed the intention to emerge from suffering and its causes, we try to make it inseparable from mind. After some time, it will become second nature or uncontrived. When a state of mind is uncontrived, it arises naturally without effort. We attain the first of the five Buddhist paths — the path of accumulation — when the intention to definitively emerge from suffering and its causes becomes second nature. A 'path' is a state of mind or mind itself; it is a realisation or meditative attainment. So to attain a path means to develop a particular state of mind to a certain fixed degree.

The intention to definitively emerge or be free from suffering and its causes is also known as renunciation. In order to develop an uncontrived sense of renunciation, we must understand the suffering that is caused by attachment to pleasures derived from karmic actions and disturbing emotions. We must also understand that it is possible to attain a type of pleasure untainted by suffering and the disturbing emotions — a pleasure that is unchanging and enduring. In short, we must understand the shortcomings of contaminated, samsaric pleasures and the advantages of liberation.

Contaminated pleasures are pleasures that arise from karmic actions and the disturbing emotions. Though we may derive some degree of pleasure from actions that we perform while under the sway of disturbing emotions, this pleasure is fleeting and unsatisfying and leads to suffering. For example, you go to a restaurant and order your favourite food. When it arrives you feel like you can't get enough; but before you know it, you've eaten too much and become sick to your stomach. It started out pleasant but became unpleasant. Or perhaps you don't overeat but before long you begin to crave for the dish and you feel unsatisfied. This is just one example of what happens when our experience of pleasure is bound by karmic actions and disturbing emotions. Things are quite different when we throw off these bindings. Without self-grasping and disturbing emotions, the experience of pleasure is free from such faults.

Someone who has developed renunciation is not attached to the pleasures of cyclic existence or samsara. Such a person does not trade reliable, deep and lasting happiness for fleeting and rather insignificant pleasures. By developing renunciation, we develop the desire to abandon contaminated pleasures as well as suffering, and to attain the happiness of liberation. We 'cultivate renunciation' by acquainting our minds with this through meditation.

The Mahayana or Great Vehicle wish for liberation includes great compassion or, more particularly, the mind of enlightenment. The mind of enlightenment or *bodhicitta* is a mind that thinks to attain buddhahood in order to free all sentient beings from suffering. A compassionate person cannot bear to stand by and do nothing about the suffering that others undergo. But equanimity must precede compassion to ensure that our compassion is unbiased and directed towards all, without exception. To build upon the foundation of equanimity and acquaint ourselves with the desire that others be free of suffering is to 'cultivate compassion'. Great compassion leads to the highest intention.

The highest intention is borne of compassion — it is the desire to do something personally to alleviate the suffering of others. Someone with the highest intention not only wishes that others do not suffer but also feels a responsibility to bring that about. Accordingly, someone with the highest intention assumes the burden of making that wish a reality.

When you assume responsibility for freeing others from suffering, you begin to wonder how you can achieve this. You then realise that, in your present state, the amount you can do for others is limited; yet if you had consummate wisdom, compassion and ability you could accomplish much more. In this way, the highest intention leads to the mind of enlightenment. The mind of enlightenment is a mind that strives to attain consummate wisdom, compassion and ability for the benefit of all beings. A person with this mind is a *bodhisattva*.

In cultivating renunciation, we see the shortcomings of samsaric pleasures and the advantages of liberation. Reflecting on the way sentient beings suffer, we feel compelled to act and aspire to buddhahood — to attain consummate wisdom, compassion and ability. We have attained the Mahayana path of accumulation when our uncontrived renunciation is qualified by an uncontrived mind of enlightenment. When you have renunciation you intend to emerge from your own suffering and its causes. When you have the mind of enlightenment you intend to attain buddhahood so you can help others do the same.

We have gone a long way towards developing the mind's ultimate nature when we develop uncontrived renunciation and an uncontrived mind of enlightenment. At that point we must try to realise the mind's ultimate nature. Neither the intention to definitively emerge nor the mind of enlightenment can cut the root of cyclic existence, the misapprehension of self. However, realising the naturally present potential

— the emptiness of mind — *will* reverse this fundamental misapprehension.

It is not easy to realise the emptiness of mind straight away. Nagarjuna taught his students to recognise the emptiness of a chariot or the 'I' before turning their attention to the emptiness of mind. The same approach is still appropriate.

Think about the emptiness of a building, for instance. The red brick structure across the street appears to be a building. We point to it saying, 'That building over there is old,' but where is the building among all that brick and mortar? The bricks themselves are not the building; neither are the mortar, pillars or crossbeams. It seems there is a building that exists from its own side, the side of the bricks and mortar. But upon investigation we find no 'building' among them. 'Building' is merely labelled onto those parts and is empty of any inherent existence. Or we might think, 'If a building is not its parts, it must be a distinct entity.' But without those parts, where is the building? So a building is also empty of any independent existence.

In brief, there is a distinct difference between what we perceive and what actually exists. It is easier to see this discrepancy in relation to coarse objects like buildings than it is with mind. We are on the verge of realising the emptiness of an object — be it mind, house or car — when we realise that it does not exist as it appears to.

Once we have realised emptiness conceptually, we must continue to acquaint ourselves with it through calm abiding and insight meditation. Calm abiding is a stable and subtle from of concentration. Like a candle buffeted by the wind, a mind blown about by distractions cannot fully illuminate an object. Calm abiding brings stability and protects the concentrated mind from distracting thoughts so that it can become more familiar with the object of meditation. Before attaining calm abiding, the meditator must develop their ability in nine stages of 'mental abiding'. As the person passes through each stage they become more skilled in focusing single-pointedly on an object of meditation. Eventually the person's body and mind become so flexible that they attain the bliss of a pliant body and mind. Calm abiding is attained once the person who can effortlessly remain on a chosen object in whichever way they please achieves this blissful pliancy.

Once calm abiding has been achieved, the meditator goes on to develop insight. Whereas calm abiding remains single-pointedly on its object, insight analyses it. Initially, this analysis threatens to disturb calm abiding, but the meditator strikes a balance by alternating between analysis and one-pointed abiding. Eventually the analysis produces even greater stability and blissful pliancy than before, and insight is achieved.

Calm abiding can be developed without meditating on

emptiness. A person could select a more simple object to focus on and only move on to emptiness once calm abiding has been attained. Once calm abiding focused on emptiness has been developed, we cultivate insight until we attain and integrate it with calm abiding. At that point we attain the second of the five paths — the path of preparation.

The process I am describing details the changes in mind that occur as it comes closer to becoming the *wisdom dharma body* of a buddha. Desirous attachment, anger and pride, along with subtle wrong consciousnesses like thinking the 'I' and other 'things' exist truly, can no longer arise once a person attains the integration of calm abiding and insight focused on emptiness. These disturbing emotions and the misapprehensions of self are called 'emotional obscurations'. They mainly prevent a person from attaining liberation. These obscurations are not abandoned by calm abiding and insight, but they are rendered impotent by the force of their attainment.

To attain the path of preparation, a person must conceptually realise emptiness. On the path of preparation a person familiarises themself with emptiness so that they can eventually perceptually realise it. In perceptually realising emptiness, a person's mind perceives emptiness, free from thought. Whereas a conceptual realisation will prevent disturbing emotions and the like from manifesting, a perceptual realisation of emptiness actually eliminates or abandons them, together with their seeds, so they cannot arise again. These obscurations are not abandoned all at once but in stages, starting with coarser levels and progressing to more and more subtle levels.

Once we have perceptually realised emptiness, we perceptually realise the emptiness of mind. This perceptual realisation is a direct antidote to disturbing emotions. The ultimate nature of mind becomes a true cessation once the levels of obscurations are abandoned. It is a true 'cessation' in that the first and most coarse level of emotional obscurations have been abandoned and therefore ceased in one's mindstream.

When emptiness is perceptually realised, the mind becomes a true path. A true path is a direct antidote to the obscurations that prevent us from attaining liberation and buddhahood. When the first level of obscuration is abandoned, the emptiness of mind becomes a true cessation. A true cessation is the emptiness of a mind in which at least one level of obscurations have completely ceased. True paths and true cessations are ultimate Dharma Jewels and the actual refuge. We find a real refuge from suffering and its causes once we develop these two. True refuge does not come from an external source but is developed from within.

A being on the bodhisattva path progresses through ten grounds or stages before reaching enlightenment.[3] As we progress through the first seven *bodhisattva grounds* we abandon the emotional obscurations and develop both mind and its emptiness. The complete abandonment of all emotional obscurations without exception occurs when the eighth ground is attained. At that point, the emptiness of mind becomes a true cessation of all emotional obscurations and their seeds, while the mind acts as the true path that effects this cessation.

The second type of obscuration is called a 'cognitive obscuration'. Cognitive obscurations are abandoned on the eighth to tenth grounds. Near the end of the tenth ground the mind itself becomes a direct antidote to the remaining cognitive obscurations. In the period that follows, the mind becomes the wisdom dharmakaya, while the emptiness of mind becomes the essential dharmakaya.

While the finer details may not be clear to you at this moment, it is important to understand that we can develop the mind by cultivating positive states of mind and strengthening our acquaintance with them. The final outcome of this process is that you develop wisdom to its utmost extent and are freed from all obscuration or delusion; the mind itself becomes an entity of consummate wisdom with absolutely no defilements.

What does developing our mind have to do with alleviating the suffering of others? Developing the mind involves developing great loving-kindness and great compassion. What is great compassion? It is a state of mind that impartially wishes that all sentient beings be free of suffering, regardless of whether they help us, harm us or have no effect on us. Of course, it is also important to act on this wish, but initially training in compassion takes precedence.

Typically, our minds are powerless, and under the sway of passing negative mental states like attachment, anger, pride, or envy. We need to gain control of the mind by training it in positive mental states like compassion, loving-kindness and patience. When we train our minds in compassion, we extend our compassion towards all beings. In doing so, we stop the attachment to those we like, the hostility to those we don't, and the neglect of those whom we are indifferent to that so often besets us.

We cannot alleviate the suffering of all beings simultaneously. Our ability to put the intention into practice is quite limited, perhaps to one person at a time. When meditating, focus on all beings. When acting, begin with those around you. Try to maintain concern for the people you come into contact with, like your circle of family and friends, your co-workers, and your neighbours, without getting angry with them. After all, what good is it to cultivate compassion on the meditation cushion if you are fighting with your family!

How do we guard the mind to avoid the risks of giving

it free rein? By applying the five powers. Upon waking up in the morning, set an intention to guard your mind. At various points of the day, check your mind. Analyse it to see how it is behaving. Which direction is it moving in: positive or negative? It is a bit like watching a small child: you always have to keep an eye on the child to make sure they do not harm themself.

Shantideva says that guarding the mind is the supreme austerity. We must pay special attention to the most harmful negative states of mind, such as anger, pride, envy and so on, and the situations that contribute to them. In being watchful, we can take greater care to prevent negative states of mind from manifesting. The intention we set in the morning is twofold. Firstly, it is a general intention to watch and guard the mind. Secondly, there is the intention to take care with specific negative states of mind that we struggle with as individuals.

All mental events, whether positive or negative, are temporary. Take anger, for instance. When anger manifests, it seems as though the mind itself becomes anger. Though the mind does not become anger, we cannot separate the two, saying, 'Here is anger and here is the mind.' Yet anger never actually permeates the nature of mind, as evidenced by the fact that anger fades while the mind remains. If you throw dust into a glass of water, the water becomes clouded and dirty. But if we put the dirty water through a filter, the water comes out clean because the filter removes the debris. Similarly, the disturbing emotions and misconceptions that obscure the mind do not permeate the nature of mind, and thus they can be removed. Disturbing emotions are based on an erroneous view of things, be it perceptual or conceptual. If we understand the way in which we have erred, the error cannot harm us and we can take steps to remove it.

I often think that our whole approach to dealing with anger is misguided. In my opinion, we should not focus on the object or person that makes us angry, but on anger itself. Look at the way anger apprehends the situation. If we can do this, we end up putting a cap on anger so that it does not continue to grow. If, on the other hand, we focus on the object or person, the anger intensifies. Looking at anger itself undermines it, whereas looking at the object of our anger strengthens and stabilises it. The same is true of attachment. If we struggle with strong attachment, we should not focus on the object that we are attached to, but on the nature of attachment itself. Of course, this is not easy, but if you try it I think you will find it beneficial.

Awakening buddha potential

Next, I will briefly explain the way to awaken our buddha potential, the signs that we have done so and the way to proceed once buddha potential has been awakened.

Buddha nature

We can awaken our buddha potential by properly going for refuge because in doing so we accumulate virtue and purify negativities. In this respect, we must not have too limited a conception of what it means to 'go for refuge'. 'Going for refuge' does not just mean to clasp one's hands in prayer and show respect to an image of the Buddha. To properly go for refuge, we must embrace the Dharma as taught in the Buddhist texts. To 'embrace the Dharma' means to understand what must be adopted and what must be abandoned. Having understood these points, we then try to develop the intention to definitively emerge, loving-kindness, and compassion; and practise the six perfections of generosity, ethics, patience, joyous effort, concentration and wisdom. This is the true meaning of 'going for refuge'.

Since the Dharma provides refuge from suffering and its causes, it is emphasised above all else. Yet in going for refuge to the Dharma we must also go for refuge to Buddha, for buddhas reveal the Dharma. Think of this example. For someone stricken by illness, it is of utmost importance to take medicine. But a properly trained doctor is also indispensable; how else will the patient know the right medicine and the way it must be administered? Just as a doctor is of secondary importance to the treatment, the Buddha is of secondary importance to the Dharma, yet is still indispensable.

'Refuge' is not only relevant to Buddhists. Refuge refers

to the techniques that actually alleviate suffering and lead one to freedom. Is merely calling out a buddha's name going to shelter us from suffering? 'Properly going for refuge' means purifying negativities and accumulating virtue; as negativities arise from mind and leave potencies behind in the mind, they must be purified by mind, not by some external source.

We must effect a transformation of mind and cultivate the intention to definitively emerge and loving-kindness and compassion. Such positive states of mind purify negative potencies and leave positive ones in their place. Since negative potencies act as causes for suffering and positive ones as causes for happiness, this approach gives us tangible shelter from suffering and its causes. Logically, it should be obvious that the Dharma is of greatest importance in going for refuge. Put simply, 'properly going for refuge' implies mind-training. Training the mind in loving-kindness and compassion awakens the buddha potential within.

The signs of having awakened buddha potential

In the *Sutra on the Ten Grounds* it is said:

> *Just as by the presence of smoke you can infer the presence of fire,*
> *And by the presence of a crane you can infer the presence of water,*

Buddha nature

*The wise are able to infer the signs of a skilled bodhisattva
Who has awakened the buddha potential.*[4]

If you look up at a mountain pass and you see smoke, you can easily infer that there must be fire up there. We know that there must be fire on the mountain pass because without fire there would be no smoke.

Similarly, we can use logic to infer that a person has awakened his or her buddha potential. If our eyes involuntarily well up with tears or the hair on our arms stands on end when studying Mahayana teachings on emptiness or the mind of enlightenment, it is a sign that we have awakened the Mahayana lineage. Certain outward physical signs might appear when we are sincerely and deeply moved by teachings on the Mahayana method and wisdom. These can be interpreted as signs that the buddha potential has been awakened.

Studying, reflecting and meditating on the teachings helps engender the physical and mental changes that indicate the awakening of buddha potential. If we take to heart and integrate whatever teachings we receive, reflecting on them in light of our own experience, we will eventually develop a genuine appreciation for the Dharma. Such genuine appreciation is one of the many mental signs of having awakened the buddha potential. If we fail to integrate the teachings, there is the danger that we fall prey to competitiveness and envy. If we fall under the sway of such disturbing emotions, we might dismiss the qualities of others and point out their faults, which is quite negative.

We gain knowledge of the Dharma to subdue the disturbing emotions and develop a good heart. If we use our knowledge of Dharma to judge, criticise and belittle others, we turn the Dharma back to front. Such mistaken tendencies are roundly scolded for they do not lead to virtue, but to non-virtue.

The mind of enlightenment

Having encouraged positive states of mind and discouraged negative ones as much as possible, we must mingle the mind with loving-kindness and compassion. Eventually, if we do so, the desire to attain consummate wisdom, compassion and ability for the benefit of all beings arises and our mind becomes the mind of enlightenment. The mind of enlightenment itself is a mind that is accompanied or assisted by two aspirations: the aspiration to enlightenment and the aspiration to alleviate the suffering of all beings. If we transform our mind into a mind of enlightenment we are doing well!

The mind of enlightenment may be contrived or uncontrived. If we take care and cultivate it properly it will eventually remain effortlessly without cultivation — uncontrived. If we take a casual approach, the mind of enlightenment will remain contrived. When we develop an uncontrived mind of enlightenment we enter the first Mahayana path, the Mahayana path of accumulation.

The uncontrived mind of enlightenment has many phases, the first three of which are the earth-like, gold-like, and crescent moon-like phases. Initially we develop the earth-like mind of enlightenment, which is likened to the earth because it is a foundation, a support for the qualities and realisations of the altruistic intention. Without care, this mind may fall from its noble intention. Next, the gold-like mind of enlightenment is developed. Just as gold remains gold despite being underground for centuries, the gold-like mind of enlightenment will not deteriorate into a less noble mind. The third phase is likened to a waxing crescent moon. According to the lunar calendar, the moon is first seen on the third day, after which it continues to wax until it becomes full and begins to wane. While waxing, the moon 'increases' without diminishing. Similarly, the crescent moon-like mind of enlightenment continues to expand and grow without any chance of diminishing.

Once we have successfully developed an uncontrived mind of enlightenment, we turn our attention to realising the emptiness of mind. If we have not done so before, we must ascertain the emptiness of mind while on the path of accumulation: first realising emptiness, then developing calm abiding and insight focused upon emptiness, and integrating them. Study and reflection are emphasised above meditation on the path of accumulation. In other words, analytical meditation takes precedence over one-pointed meditation. Then, having attained the integration of calm abiding and insight focused on emptiness and moved onto the path of preparation, meditation becomes predominant.

Of course, we need to practise single-pointed meditation, but we are still not entirely clear about the object of placement meditation — emptiness. Study and reflection are required to develop that clarity. We must distinguish between single-pointed placement meditation and analytical meditation. At this early stage we should not emphasise one-pointed placement meditation, but we should emphasise analytical meditation on emptiness.

There are four levels to the path of preparation based on the various coarse and subtle levels of misapprehending the self of persons and phenomena. As we develop, more and more subtle levels of the misapprehension of the self become inactive; that is, they are no longer able to manifest. Progress through the four levels of the path of preparation reflects this. If the root of the disturbing emotions — the misapprehension of self — cannot manifest, it is obvious that the disturbing emotions cannot either.

What is the difference between the *acquired* and the

instinctual misapprehensions of self? The acquired misapprehension of self is a misapprehension of the self that we adopt under the influence of philosophical ideas or certain reasons that we are exposed to. The instinctual misapprehension of self is a misapprehension of self that we have always been subject to through habit. The actual root of cyclic existence is the instinctual misapprehension of self. It exists in the mental continuum of all beings, even animals. The acquired misapprehension of the self will only afflict a person who has come into contact with philosophical or spiritual ideas that promote the idea of a truly existent self and so on.

Towards the end of the last level of the path of preparation, we enter into a one-pointed state of meditation called 'equipoise' in which we have our first perceptual realisation of emptiness. The moment this realisation takes place, we attain the third path, the path of seeing.

Abandoning the defilements

When we develop an uncontrived mind of enlightenment, the mind becomes a Mahayana path of accumulation. When we attain the integration of calm abiding and insight focused on emptiness, the mind becomes the path of preparation. When we perceptually realise emptiness, the mind becomes the path of seeing. Once the path of seeing is attained, the acquired misapprehension of self and its karmic seeds can no longer remain in the mind and are abandoned. For that reason, the acquired misapprehension of self along with its seeds are called 'abandonments of the path of seeing'.

An analogy might help us understand the process that renders increasingly subtle levels of the misapprehension of self ineffectual. In the middle of winter, an unheated room can become very cold. But if we put a heater in that room, the heat gradually pushes back the cold and the chill can no longer harm us. On the path of preparation, we do not rid the mind of the misapprehension of self and its seeds, but we do prevent them from manifesting. On the path of seeing, we actually begin to abandon them for good.

The initial period in which we perceptually realise emptiness is called the uninterrupted path. The second period is called the liberated path, as we are liberated from the acquired misapprehension of self and its seeds, which have ceased to exist in our mental continuum. All at once the mind becomes the liberated path of seeing, while the emptiness of mind becomes a true cessation of the acquired misapprehension of the self — the first true cessation we attain.

The person who attains the uninterrupted path of seeing perceptually realises the emptiness of mind in one-pointed equipoise. In the next period he or she attains the liberated path of seeing and a true cessation while still in one-pointed equipoise. Though the acquired misapprehension and its seeds are abandoned on the path of seeing, the instinctual misapprehension of self and its seeds must be abandoned on the fourth path, the path of meditation — in nine cycles according to the Sutra tradition. Increasingly more subtle levels of the disturbing emotions — called emotional obscurations — are abandoned as a person progresses to the eighth bodhisattva ground. From the eighth ground, the imprints left behind by the misapprehension of self are abandoned.

We proceed through the path of meditation in much the same fashion as we do the path of seeing. First we attain an uninterrupted path in which we apply the direct antidote to one level of emotional obscuration, and having abandoned them, we attain a liberated path. This occurs for each of the bodhisattva grounds until we attain the liberated path of the eighth ground. The liberated path of the eighth ground is attained together with the true cessation of all disturbing emotions — the emotional abandonments of the path of meditation.

The uninterrupted paths and liberated paths occur once each on the path of seeing and multiple times on the path of meditation, once apiece for each of the ten grounds. Each uninterrupted path acts as a direct antidote to a corresponding level of obscuration. A liberated path arises once the preceding uninterrupted path has finished abandoning the corresponding level of obscuration. The fifth path is the path of no-more-learning — buddhahood.

Abandoning the obscurations

Having abandoned the emotional obscurations, we must then abandon the cognitive obscurations, which is done in three cycles. The first cycle is abandoned when we attain the ninth ground, the second cycle is abandoned when we attain the tenth ground and the third and final cycle is abandoned when the mind transforms into the wisdom dharmakaya and all obscurations without exception are removed. When this happens, the emptiness of mind becomes the essential dharmakaya. This is the way the mind and the emptiness of mind become the wisdom dharmakaya and the essential dharmakaya respectively.

The waxing moon is an analogy for this process. The moon is first seen on the third day following a new moon. On each successive day, we are able to see a bit more, until the fifteenth day when we see a full moon. Similarly, the emptiness of mind is initially obscured by defilements. When we attain the path of seeing we remove the coarsest defilements and catch our first perceptual glimpse of the emptiness of mind. As we progress and develop our realisation of emptiness, we cleanse more and more of the defilements obscuring the mind's emptiness. Finally, we witness the full dawning of the wisdom dharmakaya free of defilements, radiant like a full moon. In other words, the emptiness of mind is gradually cleansed of defilements until it is completely cleansed and buddhahood is attained.

The minds of all sentient beings are fit to be cleansed in this way. The naturally present buddha potential is defined as 'the emptiness of a mind obscured by defilements that is fit to become the essential dharmakaya'. This definition excludes the possibility that the emptiness of a buddha's mind be considered 'buddha potential' because the emptiness of a buddha's mind is not obscured by defilements.

We have been speaking almost exclusively about the naturally present potential, but what about the buddha potential that needs to be developed? The buddha potential that needs to be developed is defined as 'a compound that is fit to become a buddha body'. Mainly this refers to the intention to definitively emerge, loving-kindness, compassion and other valid states of mind, which become the wisdom dharmakaya when developed to their utmost extent.

According to the Sutra tradition, loving-kindness, compassion and the mind of enlightenment are cultivated in order to alleviate the suffering of sentient beings. We can attain the two form bodies of the buddha — the two *rupakayas* — by cultivating them. The two form bodies are needed to accomplish the well-being of others. Neither the essential nor the wisdom dharmakaya can accomplish the benefit of others since they do not have form.

We attain the two reality bodies — the two dharmakayas — by developing the wisdom that realises emptiness and removing the defilements that obscure the emptiness of mind, thereby accomplishing our own benefit.

These two are necessary for us to fully accomplish the well-being of others since we cannot do so until we have purified our own obscurations. So in brief, we meditate on emptiness mainly to purify our own obscurations, and loving-kindness and compassion to attain the rupakayas that allow us to benefit others.

By meditating on emptiness we gather the accumulation of wisdom, which induces the two dharmakayas. By cultivating loving-kindness and compassion we gather the accumulation of merit, which induces the two rupakayas. This is how to proceed once our buddha potential has been awakened. The development of the dharmakaya depends on earlier steps, but first we must awaken our buddha potential.

PART TWO

The Three Principal Aspects of the Path

The Three Principal Aspects of the Path is one of many texts composed by Lama Tsongkhapa. Over fourteen verses Tsongkhapa teaches the three practices that are indispensable to becoming a buddha. This text was written for one of his students, and the intimacy of the teacher–student relationship is evident throughout. These lines are personal instructions, given out of a deep concern for the well-being of his student and, by extension, all sentient beings. Tsongkhapa encourages us to 'Integrate these ideas!' — testimony to their practical nature. This is not mere philosophical speculation but the very heart of Mahayana Buddhist practice. In Chapter 4, headings have been inserted for each of the fourteen verses to clarify the topics. Chapter 4 sets the historical stage for Chapters 5, 6 and 7, which introduce and explain each of the Three Principal Aspects of the Path in more detail.

The Three Principal Aspects of the Path are the very essence of the Buddha's teachings. A real taste for the Dharma develops as our study of his teachings deepens, and mind and Dharma mingle.

These teachings are very practical and applicable to our everyday lives; we can integrate and internalise them. But if we neglect in-depth study and do not bring them into our experience, we will approach the Dharma as we do the television, and the benefits will be quite limited. We cannot savour the deep and satisfying flavour of the teachings when they pass by like images on a screen.

This world is full of problems and suffering. When I fled Tibet, I left my monastery, my family and relatives; yet I have not suffered as one would expect, given these circumstances. I attribute this to my study of the Dharma and the fact that my studies have mingled with my mind. This is what the Dharma does for you. I hope that you have a similar opportunity for study, and in addition that you have some time to meditate. If, like myself, you do not devote a specific period of your life exclusively to meditation, you can still mix your mind with the Dharma. Think then of the benefits of spending more time in meditation, for surely they would be even greater!

It is my hope that you have the opportunity to learn more about the Dharma, to meditate on it and to mix your mind with it. I believe this will help you taste the Dharma so that your mind is happier and more relaxed during life and at ease and peaceful in the face of death.

4

A history of the lam rim and Gelug lineage

This chapter tells the story of two great masters and the lineage of teachings traced back to them. First, the traditional life-story of the great eleventh-century Indian master Atisha is summarised. Coming to Tibet at a historically crucial time, Atisha developed a style of instruction specifically tailored to unruly Tibetans. He presented the whole array of Buddhist teachings in a systematic way to clarify the successive stages we must go through to attain enlightenment. The stages of the path presentation, or *lam rim*, as it is known in Tibetan, was adopted by masters from all four Tibetan Buddhist schools and continues to be hugely influential to this day. One of the most important proponents of this genre was Lama Tsongkhapa, whose life-story is also outlined in this chapter. If Atisha invented the genre, Lama Tsongkhapa perfected it in his text, *The Great Treatise on the Stages of the Path to Enlightenment*. Tsongkhapa's lineage is passed on in the *Gelug* school, the order to which both His Holiness the Dalai Lama and Geshe Tashi Tsering belong.

The life of Atisha

Atisha was an Indian-born scholar who travelled widely and revived Buddhism in Tibet. He composed *A Lamp for the Path to Enlightenment* on which the lam rim, or stages of the path, teachings are based.

In 982 CE, Atisha was born the son of a king in an area now known as Bengal. His biography leaves the reader with the impression that this was a very special master, someone who had gained power over birth and death, and was not controlled by karma and disturbing emotions. From a young age, Atisha displayed a strong interest in the Buddha's teachings. The natural devotion he showed to Buddha images was only one of many signs that he enjoyed the fruits of past prayers.

As a young man, Atisha showed no interest in the wealth and court life of his family. He thought solely of seeking out a qualified guru who could teach him to practise the pure Dharma. By the age of twenty-one, he had mastered both the Buddhist teachings and traditional fields of knowledge, such as astrology and medicine. Renowned for his extensive learning, he was given the name 'Glorious' Atisha.

Atisha travelled far and wide in search of teachings. After spending years training under various masters, he developed many realisations and proceeded to the monasteries of Vikramashila and Odantapuri, near Nalanda Monastery, where he became a great teacher. By the tenth and eleventh centuries, these monasteries were renowned throughout India for the learned masters who lived and taught there.

When he was born, Buddhism in Tibet was still in a period of decline following a major persecution carried out in the ninth century. There was almost no one in Tibet whose practice encompassed both *Vinaya* and *Mantra*. (The Vinaya is composed of teachings the Buddha gave on proper ethics and discipline. It is one of the Sutra vehicle's three 'baskets' or scriptural collections; Mantra is more widely known in the West as 'Tantra' and involves more esoteric forms of meditation.) In their ignorance, Tibetans of old held the two to be like hot and cold, opposites unable to coexist. Many Tibetans felt a single person could not integrate the conduct espoused in the Vinaya with that of Mantra. As a result, practitioners of the Vinaya denigrated and looked down upon practitioners of Mantra, and vice versa, thereby creating disharmony.

A king in western Tibet, Lha Lama Yeshe Od, was keen on restoring the Buddha's teachings, but he was greatly distressed at the rampant disharmony. He concluded that the only way to overcome this misunderstanding was to invite a learned Indian master to come to Tibet and teach. To fulfil his wishes, he sent his son along with many others on an arduous journey across the Himalayas to the great monastery where Atisha lived. Their mission was twofold: some of the group were sent by the king to train as translators, while others were to return with an Indian Buddhist master.

The hardships encountered by the group en route to India were enormous; at one point the king's son was kidnapped and held for ransom. Those who made it to India encountered further difficulties, for although they had reached their destination, the climate and diet of the warm Indian plains did not suit these young men from the cool mountains of Tibet, and as a result many of the group died.

Once the remaining members of the party arrived at the great monastery, they heard of Atisha's reputation. Here was a Buddhist master learned in both Sutra and Mantra with many more inconceivable qualities. With the confidence that this was the type of master they sought, the party relayed the news of Atisha to the Tibetan king, who was extremely pleased. Finally, after much deliberation, the senior monks of the monastery agreed to let Atisha go to Tibet on the condition that he return before too long.

Upon arrival in Tibet, Atisha realised the difficulty of his task. Despite the existence of the Buddha's teachings, the Tibetans were still rather unruly. To teach the more subtle and challenging points of the doctrine would be difficult if he could not first teach them to tame their own minds. In response to requests and the situation he encountered in

Tibet, he composed the text *A Lamp for the Path to Enlightenment*, which covered the entire path of Sutra and Mantra. Throughout this brilliant work, Atisha emphasises how to tame the mind.

Of course, all of Buddha Shakyamuni's teachings are aimed at subduing the mind. But due to their depth and breadth, it was difficult for a single individual to practise them all. Atisha's great accomplishment was to structure the vast array of Buddhist teachings in a sequential order so that they could be easily applied. *A Lamp for the Path to Enlightenment* is the first lam rim, or 'stages of the path' text. In Tibet, this genre assumed a great importance, which it enjoys to this day. Like a staircase leading to the roof of a house, the lam rim is a graduated presentation of Sutra and Mantra practices that individuals must adopt in order to ascend to enlightenment.

Atisha's instructions on Sutra and Mantra helped to eliminate hostility between practitioners of the respective traditions. He dispelled the reservations people had about the purity of certain teachings by illustrating that there was no incompatibility between Vinaya and Mantra.

When the text arrived in India, the Indian masters were overjoyed. They are said to have exclaimed, 'Even in India, Atisha never gave such a teaching! Not once during his stay at Nalanda!' All agreed that the composition of such a text alone justified Atisha's visit to Tibet. Such praise was heaped on Atisha, not just by the Tibetans who invited him to the Land of Snows but by the Indians as well. He died in Tibet in 1054, without ever having returned to India.

The life of Lama Tsongkhapa

In the year 1357 Lama Tsongkhapa was born in Tsongkha, an area of Amdo in northeast Tibet. His parents were special people who had cultivated the highest altruistic wishes. While he was in his mother's womb, his parents had significant dreams indicating that the child was an emanation of the venerable *Manjushri*.

In a remote area not far from where the child was born lived a man learned in both Sutra and Mantra, the Dharma king Dondrub Rinchen. The king, who was a great yogi, was engaged in practice on his main meditational deity, *Yamantaka*. One evening, after repeated supplications, Dondrup Rinchen had a vision of Yamantaka in which the deity said, 'Next year, I will come to this land and we will meet. Until then, take care.' The king was left to wonder what this could mean, until months later he heard of the birth of the child who would later be known as Lama Tsongkhapa, 'the Lama from Tsongkha'. Upon hearing news of the child's birth and the parents' fortuitous dreams, Dondrup Rinchen thought, 'Yamantaka is the wrathful aspect of the venerable Manjushri, the embodiment of enlightened wisdom. This child will be an inconceivable Yamantaka yogi. This must be what my vision signifies.' So he sent a traditional painting of Yamantaka to Tsongkhapa's parents with a letter instructing them to raise the child with care. The people of the area heard of this and were amazed. When the child was three years old, his father took him to meet the king.

Before he reached the age of seven, Tsongkhapa took vows from the Fourth Karmapa, Rolpe Dorje, and was given the name Kunga Nyingpo. At the age of seven, with Dondrup Rinchen acting as abbot, the child was ordained as a novice monk. As Lama Tsongkhapa wanted to study, he left for Lhasa, accompanied by the Dharma king. However, before leaving he received numerous empowerments from the king and learned much about Mantra.

Tsongkhapa arrived in central Tibet in 1374. His first place of residence was the Kagyu monastery of Drigung. After completing his study of important texts such as *The Perfection of Wisdom* scriptures, Tsongkhapa acquired a reputation for his mastery of the subject. Under the guidance of the Sakya lama, the Lord Rendawa, who was to become one of his main teachers, Tsongkhapa studied Dharmakirti's *Seven Treatises on Valid Cognition*, together with their commentaries. He soon became an unparalleled master of these texts, which are the very foundations of Buddhist logic. From the Lord Rendawa, he received teachings on the great texts of Middle

A history of the lam rim and Gelug lineage

Way philosophy. Through his studies, he mastered their meaning. Then he rounded out his studies of the traditional Buddhist subjects by studying the Vinaya and *Abhidharma*.

Tsongkhapa then left for southern Tibet, where he practised at the Jampaling Temple. Though he had internalised the scriptural teachings and oral instructions then available in Tibet, certain doubts remained. His doubts focused on the meaning of the Middle Way, but included questions about some Mantra practices, such as *Guhyasamaja* and *Chakrasamvara*. Tsongkhapa concluded that he would have to go to Nalanda Monastery to resolve his doubts. So he began making preparations for a party of nine to travel to India.

In the border regions of Lhodrag, he met a Nyingma lama who told him, 'If you go to India, you will become a great *pandita*, knowledgeable in the eighteen branches of learning, but your life will be shortened and your students will have difficulties. Stay in Tibet and pray to Manjushri and he will quickly guide you.' After receiving teachings from this Nyingma master, Tsongkhapa returned to his intensive practice.

Lama Tsongkhapa did a retreat and many practices associated with Manjushri and eventually had a vision of the deity, through which he was able to dispel many doubts about crucial points in the exalted discourses; he developed a special realisation of the Middle Way. The text *In Praise of*

Dependent Arising was conceived in meditation and composed during this period. Based on the teachings he received from Manjushri, Tsongkhapa formulated his own philosophical tenets, which are known as 'the tenets of Manjushri'.

Tsongkhapa wrote in his text, *The Great Stages of Mantra*:

> *Manjushri, the sole sire of all Conquerors!*
> *With your joyful eyes, you watched over*
> *The analysis through which the profound intention of the*
>   *Conquerors was realised.*
> *Having listened to the 'supreme act of generosity',*
> *I relied on the higher deity without interruption for some time.*
> *Still, I do not leave your lotus feet,*
> *For I have no refuge other than you, Treasury of Knowledge!*
> *Bestow on me the fruits that I hope for!*

At Ratreng Monastery, Lama Tsongkhapa had visions of the Kadampa lineage lamas from Shakyamuni down to Namkha Gyaltshan, including Atisha and his successors, Dromtonpa, and the Geshes Potowa and Sharawa. Eventually Atisha said to him, 'I will help you in your great efforts on behalf of the teachings. I will help you attain enlightenment and work for the welfare of beings.' This vision appears to be the impetus behind his composition of the text *The Great Treatise on the Stages of the Path to Enlightenment*. Not long after, many of the learned and well-known masters of central Tibet requested him to compose a text on the stages of the path. Satisfied that his vision of Atisha and other masters was a good omen, he composed his famous work, *The Great Treatise on the Stages of the Path to Enlightenment*.

Later, Tsongkhapa composed many texts and his collected works take up eighteen volumes. Just looking through the texts of these eighteen volumes is enough to convince a person of Tsongkhapa's learning in both Sutra and Mantra and the breadth of his scholarship: there are texts on valid cognition, the perfection of wisdom literature, Middle Way philosophy, and the ethics of the Vinaya and Mantra. A close and detailed reading of his text *The Great Treatise on the Stages of the Path to Enlightenment* demonstrates his incredible knowledge of the Sutra teachings and his masterful understanding of the correct view of reality. This text inspires such confidence because the conclusions he reaches are accompanied by quotes from the Buddha's sutras and Indian scriptures and are supported by logic and reasoning. Anyone interested in the breadth of Lama Tsongkhapa's scholarship or how he understands a particular point of sutra can find their answer in this amazing text.

Among his many Mantra texts, *The Great Stages of Mantra* ought to convince us of his knowledge of Mantra. In short, the clearest and best evidence for Tsongkhapa's mastery of both Sutra and Mantra lie in reading *The Great Treatise on the Stages of the Path to Enlightenment* and *The Great Stages of Mantra*.

The Great Prayer Festival of Miracles

After meditating on Manjushri and recalling the great kindness of the Buddha, Lama Tsongkhapa was moved to commemorate the Buddha's miraculous deeds with a great prayer festival. The festival was timed to coincide with a holiday marking Buddha Shakyamuni's performance of a series of great miracles. Tsongkhapa had the idea to hold such a festival and make great offerings to the divine image of Buddha Shakyamuni held in the Jokhang Temple in Lhasa. Due to his fame, he was able to organise large offerings from the Tibetan faithful — enough to sponsor what came to be known as the 'Great Prayer Festival of Miracles'. As part of the extensive preparations leading up to the festival, held in the first month of the Tibetan calendar, he restored and made improvements to the temple that housed the image. The festival, which lasted two weeks, was a great success, attracting a huge assembly of monks from all over Tibet.

With offerings from the festival, Tsongkhapa had the Buddha Shakyamuni statue covered in gold leaf, and added ornaments and attire so that it assumed the aspect of the Buddha's 'complete enjoyment body'. The Buddha is usually portrayed in the aspect of his emanational body, the form he assumed in manifesting enlightenment at Bodh Gaya and turning the wheel of Dharma at Varanasi. But at the same time, the Buddha travelled secretly to Uddiyana and turned the wheel of Mantra Dharma. It was while teaching Mantra that he assumed the aspect of the complete enjoyment body. The Great Prayer Festival gave the wealthy and common folk alike a chance to accumulate merit by making offerings to improve the central temple and support a large gathering of ordained monks and nuns. Buddhists believe that prayers made by a great assembly of Sangha have added potency. Thus during the Great Prayer Festival of Miracles the people prayed that the Buddha's teaching continue to flourish without decline. This festival, held to commemorate the kindness of the Buddha, is held annually to this day.

Lama Tsongkhapa's legacy

Lama Tsongkhapa's reputation grew as people realised that the philosophical understanding he articulated was more subtle than the prevailing views of the time. Together with his influence and popularity, the number of his students swiftly increased. To provide them with a proper place for study and practice, he founded Ganden Monastery, outside Lhasa. The tradition that grew out of this monastery became known as the *Riwo Genden*, or 'Virtuous Mountain' school, which is known today simply as the *Gelug*. Later his students founded Sera and Drepung monasteries, which, together with Ganden, make up 'The Three Monastic Seats' of the Gelug order.

While maintaining the vows of a fully ordained monk, Tsongkhapa developed high realisations during his life and attained buddhahood in the state after death. He passed away in 1419, leaving behind one of the most influential bodies of work in Tibetan Buddhist history.

The Great Treatise on the Stages of the Path to Enlightenment

Of all the texts he composed, most Westerners associate Lama Tsongkhapa with the great text, *The Great Treatise on the Stages of the Path to Enlightenment*. The stages of the path are divided into three groups that accord with the scope or aims of different individuals. Thus the text, known in Tibetan as the *Lam Rim Chenmo*, presents the path to enlightenment in terms of the 'three types of being', the earlier stages acting as building-blocks for the later ones. The stages of the path are divided into the stages of the smaller, middle, and greater scope beings. These stages include the entire range of techniques required to attain buddhahood. In that sense, *The Great Treatise on the Stages of the Path to Enlightenment* is a guidebook that teaches how practitioners develop realisations of the path.

Much of what is studied in Tibetan Buddhism can be found in the stages of the path held in common with a being of middle scope. When training in those stages, we can consult Lama Tsongkhapa's text to see what comes next and how we should proceed in order to progress. This is one of the great values of such a work; it reads like a map. *The Great Treatise on the Stages of the Path to Enlightenment* is a guide that illustrates the proper sequence and landmarks for all the stages of our spiritual journey.

Though there are many texts belonging to the lam rim genre, Tsongkhapa's is the most important and proper study of it is sure to have an impact. A person cannot help but be moved by its citations of the Buddha's words. This approach instils confidence that there is a sound source for Tsongkhapa's teachings.

Over and over again, Tsongkhapa quotes the great Indian pioneers and explains the logic and reasoning behind the teachings. When a person gives you directions to a certain place, the directions reveal the route, nothing else. *The Great Treatise on the Stages of the Path to Enlightenment* not only shows the route to buddhahood, it also demonstrates the purpose for embarking on such a journey and gives evidence that proves the accuracy of the directions. Its use of scriptural quotation and logic is a powerful method for cutting the doubts we harbour about the path.

Beings of the Three Scopes

A being of the greatest or highest scope seeks to use this life to actualise buddhahood. To that end, such a person emphasises the practices of loving-kindness, compassion and the mind of enlightenment, while cultivating the correct view. Though such a person does develop the wisdom realising emptiness, his or her main practice is aimed at overcoming self-cherishing, that is, self-centred indifference to the plight of others.

A being of the middling scope does not want to suffer even in the slightest. Thus, with thoughts of his or her own welfare, such a person seeks to attain a state of liberation totally free from suffering and its causes. While maintaining a practice focused upon emptiness, this person's main practice revolves around renunciation, that is, the wish to definitively emerge from cyclic existence into a state of freedom. This type of being's chief concern is with applying an antidote to his or her attachment to contaminated pleasures.

A being of the lesser scope tries to secure a pleasant rebirth in future lives. While a greater scope being strives for enlightenment and a middle scope being strives for liberation, this person aims only to attain rebirth as a human in successive lives. This is the most limited — or most short-sighted — of the three orientations. As there are three different goals pursued by the three different types of beings, three different paths are taught to them. Beings of the greatest scope are taught the importance of the mind of enlightenment and the correct view. In addition to training in the stages of small and medium scope beings, they are encouraged to overcome their indifference to others and to cherish them. They are taught to practise the six perfections.

Beings of the middle scope seek liberation from cyclic existence, so they are taught to cultivate renunciation and the correct view. Like greater scope beings, their path must include meditation upon the correct view, for liberation is impossible without the wisdom that realises emptiness. The main paths they practise are the three trainings in ethics, concentration and wisdom. Beings of the lesser scope seek pleasant rebirths. They are chiefly taught the path of practising virtue and abandoning non-virtue, as the cause for pleasant rebirths is virtue and the cause of unpleasant rebirths is non-virtue. The main paths of practice for this type of being are adopting the ethics of abandoning the ten non-virtues and acting as wholesomely as one is able.

If it suits us, practising the teachings of Mahayana Buddhism is of greatest importance. Bodhisattvas and buddhas are the principal role models for this type of practice: the practice of greater scope beings. The life stories of Shakyamuni before he became a Buddha provide excellent examples of how we can apply these teachings.

The Three Principal Aspects of the Path by Lama Tsongkhapa

The root text

> I prostrate to all venerable lamas.

Author's promise to compose the text

1   I will explain as well as I am able
    The essential meaning of the Conqueror's teaching,
    The path praised by all the holy children of the Conquerors,
    The only access for fortunate beings desiring highest liberation.

Author's advice to fortunate beings
to listen well and sincerely

2   Fortunate ones, listen with a pure mind!
    Do not be attached to samsaric pleasures
    And work to make your precious human rebirth meaningful.
    Set your mind to the path that pleases the Conquerors.

The reasons we need renunciation

3   Without pure renunciation there is no way to stop
            chasing after
    Pleasurable things within the ocean of samsara.
    Beings with bodies are totally bound by their thirst
            for existence
    So, please, practise renunciation from the start.

How to practise renunciation

4   *A precious human rebirth is difficult to find; there's not much time in this life.*
    Getting used to these facts will stop infatuation with this life.
    If you reflect again and again on the unfailing effects of action
    And the sufferings of samsara, infatuation with future lives will also stop.

Explaining the nature of renunciation

5   *When, through familiarity, the wish for the highest pleasures of samsara*
    Does not arise for even a single moment
    And all the time, day and night, you aim for liberation,
    Renunciation has truly been born.

Why we need to achieve bodhicitta

6   *Unless it's driven by pure bodhicitta,*
    Renunciation will never become a cause
    For the perfect happiness of highest enlightenment.
    Therefore intelligent beings cultivate supreme bodhicitta.

The method for achieving bodhicitta

7 Carried away by the torrents of four fierce rivers;
   Bound by tight fetters of karma, difficult to undo;
   Caught up in the iron net of self-grasping;
   Completely enveloped by the pitch-black darkness of ignorance.

8 In a never-ending cycle, in birth after birth,
   They're tormented without a break by the three types
       of suffering;
   By thinking about the plight of mother sentient beings
   In circumstances like these, develop the supreme mind.

Why we need correct view

9 If you don't have wisdom realising the way things are,
   Even though you familiarise yourself with renunciation and
       bodhicitta
   You won't be able to cut the root of samsara.
   So use every means to realise interdependence.

Meaning of correct view

10 When you see that for all phenomena in samsara and nirvana
   Cause and effect is unfailing
   And the object of fixation perishes,
   That is when you've entered the path that pleases the buddhas.

Incomplete correct view

11   Appearances — dependent arisings — are unfailing
       And emptiness is free of assertions.
       As long as these two seem to you disparate
       You have not yet realised the intent of Shakyamuni.

Complete correct view

12   At some point in time, suddenly, they cease to alternate
       And just by seeing that interdependence is unfailing
       A certainty that destroys all misapprehensions comes about.
       At that time your analysis of the view is complete.

13   Furthermore, appearances clear away the extreme of
           existence and
       Emptiness clears away the extreme of non-existence.
       When you understand how emptiness shows itself as
           cause and result
       You can never be held captive by extreme views.

14   When you realise as I have the crux
       Of the three principal aspects of the path explained here,
       Then, my child, stay in isolation, persevere with joy and
       Quickly accomplish the perfect goal that lies ahead.

5

Renunciation: the intention to definitively emerge

The first of the three principal aspects is renunciation, or more literally 'the intention to definitively emerge'. The connotations of 'renunciation' in the English language do not capture the essence of what this term means in Buddhism. A person does not need to renounce material possessions to develop renunciation. In Buddhism, renunciation is a state of mind; accordingly, the focus is on our internal attitudes, not external objects. Developing renunciation is really about developing a wish for stable, everlasting happiness.

We all seek pleasure and happiness, yet happiness comes in many forms. It is important to distinguish between unreliable short-term happiness and a deep and satisfying happiness. Having recognised the difference, we may shift our emphasis from the one to the other. To develop renunciation we must see things for what they are. A person who has renunciation sees the good and bad of unreliable pleasures. Seeing that, a person remains unattached to lesser pleasures and aims for the highest forms of happiness — the happiness found in the liberated state of true freedom.

This chapter covers verses 1 to 5 of *The Three Principal Aspects of the Path*, which are reproduced at the beginning of the chapter.

Verses 1 to 5 of
The Three Principal Aspects of the Path
The source verses

> *I prostrate to all venerable lamas.*

Author's promise to compose the text

1   *I will explain as well as I am able*
    The essential meaning of the Conqueror's teaching,
    The path praised by all the holy children of the Conquerors,
    The only access for fortunate beings desiring highest liberation.

Author's advice to fortunate beings to listen well and sincerely

2   *Fortunate ones, listen with a pure mind!*
    Do not be attached to samsaric pleasures
    And work to make your precious human rebirth meaningful.
    Set your mind to the path that pleases the Conquerors.

The reasons we need renunciation

3   *Without pure renunciation there is no way to stop chasing after*
    Pleasurable things within the ocean of samsara.
    Beings with bodies are totally bound by their thirst for existence
    So, please, practise renunciation from the start.

How to practise renunciation

4   A precious human rebirth is difficult to find; there's not much time in this life.
    Getting used to these facts will stop infatuation with this life.
    If you reflect again and again on the unfailing effects of action
    And the sufferings of samsara, infatuation with future lives will also stop.

Explaining the nature of renunciation

5   When, through familiarity, the wish for the highest pleasures of samsara
    Does not arise for even a single moment
    And all the time, day and night, you aim for liberation,
    Renunciation has truly been born.

> *In a Buddhist sense, renunciation does not mean that we give everything up to live as a pauper. Rather, we renounce suffering and its causes so that we can attain the lasting and unchanging happiness of liberation.*

Renunciation

Renunciation, the mind of enlightenment and the correct view are the Three Principal Aspects of the Path. They contain the very essence of the Buddha's teachings.

Renunciation [*nge jung gi bsam pa*] translates more accurately as 'the intention to definitively emerge'. This Buddhist concept is quite different from the way we normally understand the word 'renunciation'. In English, we often associate renunciation with a frugal life. It conjures up images of living like a beggar, without money or material possessions. But here renunciation means something quite different. According to Buddhism, renunciation is a state of mind; a mental attitude that is just as accessible to someone with money and material possessions as it is to someone with absolutely nothing. We need to adjust our understanding of this term if we are to understand these teachings.

When we speak of 'the intention to definitively emerge' we are not talking about wanting to live like a beggar; we are talking about wanting to emerge from suffering and its causes, for good.

Evidence for this is found in the story of an early Tibetan master, a layperson known as the Lord Marpa. Lord Marpa is most popularly known as the great teacher of Milarepa, a great Tibetan yogi. Marpa was actually a householder, not a monk; he had a wife and he kept animals to help with the farm work and to provide dairy products. Marpa clearly had both renunciation and a mind of enlightenment. A householder *can* have these things. Renunciation does not mean that we cannot have a partner or spouse, or that we cannot live like 'an ordinary person'. The fact that Marpa was a farmer and kept cows and other animals shows that we do not have to live as a beggar either.

The first line of *The Three Principal Aspects of the Path* reads:

I prostrate to all venerable lamas.

A learned person could talk for a long time about this line alone. For instance, this one line can be read as an explanation of the proper way to rely on a spiritual teacher, the first topic in the lam rim (the stages of the path). Our interest here

Renunciation: the intention to definitively emerge

though is to draw out the very essence of these teachings. We are trying to understand the text and the main points it discusses.

The ultimate aim for someone on the path is to attain buddhahood. This is a state of consummate wisdom, compassion and ability. Although the ultimate aim is buddhahood, there is also a lesser result, known as liberation. So there are basically two ways to progress along the path. We can aim towards liberation and then, after a short spell in the peace beyond sorrow, proceed to buddhahood; or we can aim straight for buddhahood, in which case liberation is attained incidental to buddhahood.

A lama is someone who completely and unerringly teaches the paths that lead to liberation and buddhahood. In doing so this person demonstrates unsurpassable kindness. Lama is a contraction of the Tibetan *lana mepa*, meaning 'unsurpassable' or 'the highest'. Lamas are unsurpassable in their kindness to us because they teach us the way to eliminate all suffering and attain the highest happiness. Many people are kind to us — our parents and teachers, for instance — but the kindness of the lama exceeds even them.

The word lama also refers to Buddha Shakyamuni, the Conqueror. Buddha Shakyamuni is the very root source of these teachings, which explain the unmistaken paths to attain liberation and buddhahood. Drawing on his own experience,

Buddha Shakyamuni unerringly taught the way to attain these two states, and so he is also included in this praise.

The word 'to prostrate', *chaktsel*, is made up of two syllables. *Chak* means 'to sweep away'. When we say, 'I prostrate to the high and holy lamas,' in essence we are requesting the lamas to sweep away the obstacles that could hinder the attainment of our goals. *Tsel* means to seek or to search — we are looking for something. It also implies a request — we are pleading with the lama, 'Please! Quickly teach us the means to actualise liberation and buddhahood.' So 'to prostrate' means to sweep away the obstacles and bestow the instructions for attaining our goal. These instructions include teaching renunciation, the mind of enlightenment and the correct view.

We have identified two goals or aims. The final goal is buddhahood, a state of consummate wisdom, consummate compassion and consummate ability. The mind of enlightenment is especially related to this since we cannot attain buddhahood without developing a mind of enlightenment. The other goal is liberation. Renunciation is especially related to this lesser goal since we cannot attain liberation without renunciation. The correct view is needed for both liberation and buddhahood.

If we think to pursue liberation first and only then go on to attain buddhahood, we must integrate renunciation and the correct view. If we think to head straight for the final

Renunciation: the intention to definitively emerge

goal, buddhahood, then we need to integrate the mind of enlightenment and the correct view.

Renunciation is included in the mind of enlightenment as a matter of course. However, the mind of enlightenment is not necessarily a by-product of renunciation. The attainments of the Buddhist path require renunciation, a mind of enlightenment and correct view.

Take this fundamental advice to heart. As you read and study the teachings, consider how they illustrate this. Reflect on this: renunciation is necessary for liberation; a mind of enlightenment is necessary for buddhahood; without the wisdom that realises emptiness — the correct view — neither of those is possible. You will come to see the connection between these teachings.

We begin with the first verse, which reads:

> *I will explain as well as I am able*
> *The essential meaning of the Conqueror's teaching,*
> *The path praised by all the holy children of the Conquerors,*
> *The only access for fortunate beings desiring highest liberation.*

The Buddha Shakyamuni is one of many beings that have conquered all obscurations without exception and gained the title Conqueror. He gave an immense number of teachings, so many that his teachings would fill eighty-four thousand volumes. The essential meaning of all eighty-four thousand is contained in the three principal aspects of renunciation, the mind of enlightenment and the correct view. This is why the second line reads:

The essential meaning of the Conqueror's teaching,

The third line explains that renunciation, the mind of enlightenment and correct view are:

The path praised by all the holy children of the Conquerors,

Those beings that have understood, experienced and applied these teachings are the holy children of the Conquerors.

Such beings are disciples of the Buddha. These disciples highly praise the path of renunciation, the mind of enlightenment and correct view, saying that a person cannot attain buddhahood without them. These three aspects are praised as the highest path, the heart of the path and the essential meaning of all the teachings given by the Buddha.

'The fortunate beings desiring liberation' and 'children of the Conquerors' are basically synonyms for a bodhisattva. The phrase 'children of the Conquerors' is sometimes translated as 'sons of the Conquerors'. This translation has led some people to conclude that Tibetans are sexist, but that is not at all the case. If you ask a Tibetan who really understands Dharma, they will explain that this phrase could not possibly refer solely to males. If you assert that it should be translated as sons, you're essentially saying that to be a bodhisattva you need to be a male, and who would assert that?

Logic, as well as quotes from different texts, prove that it is not gender specific. As soon as a person develops an uncontrived mind of enlightenment they are called a 'child of the Conquerors'; that is, a bodhisattva. Anyone who develops an uncontrived mind of enlightenment is a child of the Conquerors.

There are two types of liberation: mere liberation and unsurpassable liberation. Mere liberation refers to liberation or nirvana, the peaceful state beyond sorrow. Unsurpassable liberation refers to buddhahood. Fortunate ones seek the highest liberation, so the fourth line refers to bodhisattvas, who pursue this path while developing a mind of enlightenment.

The word 'access' refers to a river ford. Located at a low or dry point of a river, a ford gives access to the other shore. These days there are many ways to cross a body of water, but this was not always so. If a river had only a single bridge or ford, anyone wanting to cross would have to cross at that point. In a similar way, when a person wants to cross to the far shore of unsurpassable liberation — buddhahood — they must find the ford of renunciation, the mind of enlightenment and the correct view.

'I will explain as well as I am able' is a promise made by the author, Lama Tsongkhapa. He seems to be saying 'it's difficult to explain things as they really are, but I'll do my best.' With this humble promise, Lama Tsongkhapa shows his lack of pride.

The second verse reads:

> *Fortunate ones, listen with a pure mind!*
> *Do not be attached to samsaric pleasures*
> *And work to make your precious human rebirth meaningful.*
> *Set your mind to the path that pleases the Conquerors.*

This verse is meant to inspire in us the desire to listen to these teachings. The lines themselves point to a certain potential the teachings are meant to draw out of us.

Buddha did not say happiness is unnecessary, for that is not the case. We can enjoy pleasure and still practise the Dharma to eliminate the causes of suffering. In fact, we could not practise Dharma if we were utterly devoid of happiness and completely overwhelmed by suffering. Pleasures may be important, but our understanding of and attitude towards them is even more so. These lines are not so much a com-

Renunciation: the intention to definitively emerge

mand as an encouragement to see the distinction between the pleasures of samsara and liberation. For someone who is unattached to the pleasures of samsara is 'one who strives to make this precious human rebirth meaningful'. Such a person knows the value of a human life and does not fritter it away in meaningless pursuits. Rather, he or she will use this life to achieve something great, buddhahood, liberation or at least another perfect human rebirth in the future.

Samsara is a Sanskrit word meaning 'cyclic existence'. People commonly think that cyclic existence refers to the world around them. Certainly, the external environment is linked to and created by our actions, but it is not cyclic existence itself. Properly understood, mountains, trees and meadows are actually the sites in which cyclic existence takes place. Each one of us has our own cyclic existence.

Basically, cyclic existence refers to the contaminated body and mind that perpetuate further uncontrolled states. Saying that our body and mind are 'contaminated' means that actions and disturbing emotions control the processes that led to our assumption of them. It also implies that they can inflame further disturbing emotions. We did not choose to be reborn in a particular time and place; rather, actions and disturbing emotions dictated that it would be so. We do not choose to age at a certain rate or become ill at certain times or to suffer, just as we do not choose the time and circumstances of our death. These are beyond our control. Actions and disturbing emotions control us and they control the circumstances of our existence. Powerlessly, we go from life to life, body to body. Cyclic existence is characterised by this lack of control and so it is described as an uncontrolled state of existence.

When we say that cyclic existence refers to aggregates that are bound by actions and disturbing emotions and perpetuate contamination, we are identifying it with the 'places' through which we cycle. There is another way to describe cyclic existence, which identifies it with the action of cycling. In this second explanation, cyclic existence is said to be the powerless and repeated conceptions that are controlled by actions and disturbing emotions.

Pleasures that are controlled by actions and disturbing emotions are samsaric pleasures. They are unreliable because they are subject to change. What begins as pleasurable eventually becomes tiresome or even uncomfortable. If we have the sense to stop before a pleasure becomes unpleasant, before long we begin to crave it again. If we overindulge, the pleasure itself turns to displeasure.

The problem does not lie in the pleasure so much as the fact that they, like us, are controlled by actions and disturbing emotions. If we were to abandon disturbing emotions and their seeds, our pleasure and happiness would not be so unreliable.

Renunciation: the intention to definitively emerge

In fact, it would be unchanging and perfect. Having abandoned suffering and what causes it, the pleasant would not become unpleasant and we would enjoy the pleasure of liberation.

By nature, samsaric pleasures are sullied by suffering, whereas the pleasure of liberation is not. Knowing this, buddhas encourage us to seek the pleasure of liberation. This does not mean that we must reject pleasant experiences or live austere lives barren of pleasure. Rather, we should not be attached to samsaric pleasures and they should not be our main focus. There is nothing wrong with pursuing pleasant activities, but if we pursue samsaric pleasures to the exclusion of all else we will never be freed from suffering.

Samsaric pleasures are inextricably linked to suffering. If we want to be free from suffering, we must give up our attachment to samsaric pleasures. Unaware that perfect happiness exists, we may pursue lesser imperfect pleasures. Unable to taste perfect happiness, we may believe that our unreliable happiness is all there is. Wanting happiness, as all sentient beings do, we cling to what samsaric pleasures we do have and begin to exaggerate their appeal. Our attachment prevents us from seeing the possibility for perfect happiness and so we neglect to pursue it.

We naturally want to be happy and do not want to suffer. There is nothing wrong with this. However, we must recognise that there are different types of pleasure. Samsaric pleasures are unreliable and inextricably linked to suffering. The pleasure of liberation is unchanging and peaceful. If we are attached to and single-mindedly pursue unreliable pleasures to the exclusion of all else, we can never be free of suffering.

Since we are unable to experience the pleasure of liberation right now, we can enjoy what pleasures we do have, but without attachment! Do not overestimate them. Do not attribute to them qualities above and beyond what they actually possess. And lastly, do not make them your sole pursuit; remember the possibility for perfect happiness and make that your goal.

The last line of the verse reads, 'Set your mind to the path that pleases the Conquerors.' As I stated before, the 'Conquerors' is an epithet for buddhas. Buddhas are beings that have freed themselves from all fear and assume responsibility for teaching others the way to free themselves from suffering. Buddhas teach these ways to everyone without a sense of closeness to some and distance from others.

What is a path that pleases the Conqueror buddhas? A Conqueror does not want people to be too taken by samsaric pleasures. Since a Conqueror wants the best for all, a Conqueror is pleased when a person aims to attain the highest happiness of liberation and buddhahood. The path this person practises is a path that pleases the Conquerors. Those of pure mind — 'the fortunate ones' — do not crave samsaric pleasures to the exclusion of all else; they set their sights on the paths to liberation.

We don't always know if our actions will please the Conquerors. For instance, traditionally flowers and water are offered to please buddhas. But what if the person making the offering did not have a good motivation? Would it still please the buddhas? Probably not, because the buddhas are not pleased by the offerings per se but by the purity of a person's motives. The person may think they are pleasing the Conquerors when actually that is not so.

The first line says 'listen with a pure mind'. How do we know what a pure mind is? Having a pure mind means that you are not deceitful in your intentions. It means being honest, straightforward and objective. If we listen to the teachings motivated by pride, envy or any other disturbing emotion, our mind is not pure. Our motivation would not be upright. It is extremely important that our intentions be honest and not deceitful. Then we may truly listen with a pure mind.

Why we need renunciation

The third verse discusses the need to develop renunciation, the intention to definitively emerge.

> *Without pure renunciation there is no way to stop chasing after Pleasurable things within the ocean of samsara.*

> *Beings with bodies are totally bound by their thirst for existence*
> *So, please, practise renunciation from the start.*

The 'ocean of samsara' is the ocean of cyclic existence. In the middle of the ocean you cannot see either shore, just as in the midst of cyclic existence you cannot see a beginning or an end. However, that does not mean there is no end — we just have not reached it. But why?

We are very much wrapped up in our samsaric experiences, unaware that there are more reliable forms of happiness. Oblivious, we constantly long for further samsaric states and so our wish to become free of them is not very strong. Yet we cannot hope to free ourselves without overcoming our single-minded pursuit of samsaric pleasures.

What exactly are the 'pleasurable things within the ocean of samsara'? They are the temporary and unreliable happinesses that actions and disturbing emotions can offer us. If a person wants only one thing and works to achieve that and nothing else, is he or she not bound to that? Just so, our pursuit of samsaric pleasures alone binds us to a cyclic existence. How can we hope to be free from a state we are always pursuing?

If a person recognised the drawbacks of what they had, until now, pursued to the exclusion of all else, would they not have a chance to cast off their bondage? By the same token,

Renunciation: the intention to definitively emerge

if we recognise the drawbacks of samsaric pleasures we may loosen the grip of attachment enough to begin striving for liberation. In this way, we can develop the intention to definitively emerge from cyclic existence without having to deny ourselves all pleasure. This is not possible if samsaric pleasures are our sole priority.

If we really want to achieve lasting and reliable happiness, we must recognise the shortcomings of pleasures controlled by disturbing emotions and the actions they motivate. We are less likely to exaggerate their appeal if we are familiar with their drawbacks and limitations. If we know that there are more enduring and reliable forms of happiness, we are less likely to make them our sole priority. We will understand their nature more completely and will not be as trapped by them.

Knowing that the way we pursue pleasures affects the happiness and satisfaction we derive from them makes us more conscientious about the way we pursue them. For instance, everyone needs money to get by. If it is acquired through stealing and deception, we might derive some pleasure from our 'earnings' but in the long run such behaviour will bring us more grief than happiness. Even if we do not shun the pursuit of pleasure altogether, we are more careful and considerate of what we are doing.

Please don't misunderstand. Even *arhats*, practitioners who have abandoned suffering and its causes, pursue pleasure.

The desire for a peaceful pleasure, free of suffering and disturbing emotions, is what drove them to become an arhat in the first place. That desire for peace, together with an understanding of the unreliability of samsaric pleasures, is what allows them to practise so diligently. If our pursuit of pleasure is compatible with liberation it will eventually yield such results.

If we are going to strive for liberation we must ask ourselves, 'Is it possible to attain liberation? Is it even possible to eliminate suffering altogether?' To find an answer we must identify what the causes of liberation and suffering are. If you assemble all the necessary causes for a thing, it is bound to arise. That is a basic principle of cause and effect. And if you eliminate the cause for something it will be eliminated as a matter of course. This is how cause and effect works. So the real question is, 'Can we assemble the causes for liberation and abandon the causes for suffering?'

My own study of *The Three Principal Aspects of the Path* has given me the confidence that it is possible. I think it will become apparent to you once you have learned more about the intention to definitively emerge, the mind of enlightenment and the correct view.

What exactly does 'an uncontrived intention to definitively emerge' mean? It is a sense of renunciation that arises naturally without effort. It is not artificial; it is uncontrived. It is developed by repeatedly meditating on its focal objects

Renunciation: the intention to definitively emerge

—— the shortcomings of cyclic existence and the benefits of liberation. As we do so, we begin to engender the wish in our minds. As it remains manifest for longer and longer periods we become more and more familiar with it until eventually it becomes like second nature, or 'uncontrived'.

Only positive aspects of mind can be 'uncontrived', but negative states like anger are almost uncontrived in that they arise effortlessly. Anger arises effortlessly because we are so well acquainted with it. It stands to reason then that, with deep and repeated familiarity, a more positive aspect of mind, like loving-kindness or compassion, will also arise effortlessly. If anger arises simply through contact with an object, then with sufficient familiarity renunciation and a mind of enlightenment can too.

It is essential that we develop the intention to definitively emerge, a mind of enlightenment and the correct view. But first we must understand each one, lest we waste time cultivating the wrong thing!

The last two lines of the third verse read:

Beings with bodies are totally bound by their thirst for existence
So, please, practise renunciation from the start.

To 'thirst for existence' is to be attached to conditioned or cyclic existence. We thirst for its pleasures, not its sufferings. But the two are inseparable, inextricable, so pursuing the one amounts to pursuing the other. We unwittingly chase what we want to avoid! Not wanting to relinquish the pleasant, we cannot get rid of the unpleasant because the two are linked. We may not realise it but the pursuit of such pleasures is a hindrance to our desire to be free of suffering.

Attachment prevents us from seeing the shortcomings of our present state, which in turn fosters a certain complacency. Attachment does not allow us to see that the single-minded pursuit of samsaric pleasures only bolsters the suffering. If we do not recognise it as a fetter, how are we to throw it off? The other factors that bind us to cyclic existence more obviously hamper us and our desire to be free. Attachment is more tricky and elusive.

But until liberation, the only pleasures available to us are samsaric ones. How can we be unattached to them while still experiencing them? Must we go without them? Is the only way to be unattached to pleasure to go without them? No, not at all. Not having any pleasure or happiness can sometimes be an obstacle. As ordinary sentient beings, we need both pleasure and the material resources that support it. Getting rid of your car does not necessarily help you get rid of samsara! After all, the car is not samsara, is it?

In other words, being unattached does not mean giving everything up anymore than renunciation does. Attachment

Renunciation: the intention to definitively emerge

binds us by preventing us from seeing a thing as it is. Attachment exaggerates the appeal of an object and prevents us from seeing its faults. By the same logic, then, being unattached means that we must not attribute positive qualities to objects above and beyond what they actually possess.

We must think carefully about the language and terms being used. Some of these words, like attachment and renunciation, have unwanted associations. They have a very specific meaning in Buddhism, and this often differs from the way they are used in everyday language. If we did not know better, we might think that being unattached means being indifferent and renunciation means giving everything up!

The same is true with 'samsara' or cyclic existence. It is very important that we accurately identify what 'cyclic existence' really is; a vague understanding is not enough. Specifically, it refers to the body and mind aggregates that form the basis for the cycle of rebirths. More generally, it describes powerless states of existence that are controlled by actions and disturbing emotions. In freeing ourselves from cyclic existence we free ourselves from the yoke of actions and disturbing emotions. We free ourselves from the uncontrolled existence conditioned by past actions and disturbing emotions, not existence altogether!

Once we have conquered actions and disturbing emotions, we can take control of our body and mind. Then our body and mind are no longer contaminated. We gain complete power over body and mind, we do not get rid of them entirely; they are, after all, the aggregates of our being. Without a mind, there is no 'me'!

Think of cyclic existence as an electrical appliance, like a ceiling fan. The fan's blades spin when you flip the switch on the wall and the electrical current comes through. The fan by itself is powerless. The fan itself does not control its spin. It is the electricity that is sent to the fan by flicking the switch that controls the fan. If the switch was broken or if there was an electrical failure, this fan would be unable to spin itself. Just like a fan powered by electricity, cyclic existence is powered by actions and disturbing emotions. Under their influence we take rebirth after rebirth and are powerless over our birth, ageing, illnesses and death.

Tsongkhapa advises that we not be attached to samsara. Yet if asked, we might say, 'I'm *not* attached to powerless states.' So what are we attached to? We are attached to the pleasures and happiness of samsara. It is not that we do not recognise our lack of control; that is not the problem. It is obvious that we do not have total control over our happiness — it comes and goes despite our wishes to the contrary. We know this but we are still attached. So we need to apply this knowledge. If we want lasting happiness free of suffering, we must not make samsaric pleasures our sole priority. Our main goal should be the pleasures of liberation. It is important that we distinguish between the two. It is like this: suppose someone poured poison into a bowl of soup during its preparation. If we eat the soup we are certain to suffer. If we eat the soup we ingest the poison, there is no way around it. We cannot separate the harmful poison from the nourishing soup because the poison has infused the entire soup. If we do not want the suffering that comes from being poisoned, we must not eat the soup.

Attachment to samsara is like this. Although we may not be attached to the unpleasant aspects of samsara — the poison and the illness that ensues — we are attached to the pleasurable aspects — its pleasant taste. These pleasurable aspects of samsara are inextricably linked with the unpleasant aspects, so as long as we partake of one we partake of the other. There is no denying that there is pleasure within samsara and no denying that we experience this in an uncontrolled manner. Yet with the one comes the other, a situation that our attachment blinds us to.

Since attachment to samsara binds beings to it, we should seek renunciation from the outset. Proper renunciation is based on an understanding of samsara's shortcomings and an appreciation of liberation's benefits. It is not so much a wholesale rejection of pleasure as it is a deep understanding of the different types of happiness and what they offer. Not all forms of happiness are samsaric happiness; that is only one type. By nature it is uncontrolled and leads to suffering, which is why it is samsaric. There are other non-samsaric types of happiness, for instance the happiness of liberation.

Attachment to samsaric pleasures is the main obstacle that prevents us from becoming free of samsara. It creates another obstacle; it stops us from striving for liberation. To be free from samsara we must abandon our attachment to samsara and seek the happiness of liberation, thereby eliminating the two main obstacles that prevent our freedom.

There are two forms of attachment to the pleasures of samsara. We can be attached to the pleasures of this life and we can be attached to the pleasures of future lives. To overcome attachment towards the pleasures of this life we must reflect on the fourth verse:

> *A precious human rebirth is difficult to find; there's not much time in this life.*
> *Getting used to these facts will stop infatuation with this life.*
> *If you reflect again and again on the unfailing effects of action*
> *And the sufferings of samsara, infatuation with future lives will also stop.*

To 'stop' infatuation with this life means to stop the fantasies we have about it. Since we have a 'precious human rebirth' we should take advantage of it and make our lives truly meaningful. There are three subjects covered in this section. Firstly, a life in which you enjoy leisure and fortune can be made very meaningful; secondly, such an opportunity is very difficult to find; and thirdly, we do not have much time in this life. The fact that life is not long can be broken down into three components. These involve reflecting on the thought that death is certain, the time of death is uncertain and at the time of death nothing but our spiritual practice is of benefit.

Our human life is so special compared to the different life forms we can think of. We human beings are unique in our ability to evaluate and make judgements. No other animal has quite the rational mind that we do. Humans enjoy a very special opportunity: in addition to being able to discern and analyse, they possess the eight leisures and ten endowments. These eighteen leisures and endowments are internal and external conditions that are conducive to liberation.

The 'external conditions' include having free time and living in an environment conducive to the pursuit of liberation. If another person controls you, if you have so much wealth that you have absolutely no free time, or if you are suffering greatly from an illness that prevents you from using what you have, the external conditions of your life would not promote or support efforts to attain liberation.

The 'internal conditions' include our way of thinking. A person who investigates the difference between the happiness of liberation and the happiness of samsara — who thinks about the purpose of becoming free from samsara and how this is achieved — enjoys the internal conditions conducive to the attainment of liberation.

A human who enjoys all external and internal conditions conducive to liberation 'possesses the eighteen leisures and endowments'. If we were to compare the number of people who enjoy all the internal and external conditions conducive to attaining liberation with the total number of people, we would find that those who do not enjoy such conditions far outnumber those who do. Since a human life with such conditions is so rare, in terms of sheer numbers, the leisures and endowments are 'difficult to find'. What's more, this human life is a result. It is rare and difficult to find because the causes that lead to such a result are difficult to assemble. The causes for rebirth as a human replete with the leisures and endowments are very particular and special. Being difficult to fully collect, the result they produce is correspondingly rare. Such an opportunity is rare yet valuable. To obtain such an opportunity, we must be sure to fulfil the following internal conditions.

It is of utmost importance that we investigate the causes of samsara and suffering, the way to be rid of both and what needs to be adopted and discarded along the way. Investigating these and distinguishing between what is good and bad, right and wrong, correct and incorrect is very important. It is not only possible to completely eliminate our own suffering; we can also develop the ability to effortlessly and spontaneously accomplish the well-being of others. This is the most meaningful state of all, yet in order to achieve it we must have all the internal and external conditions. The internal conditions are particularly important.

This human life can be so meaningful; it is more valuable than millions of dollars. A person might have millions of dollars but if they lack these external and internal conditions they will not be able to effortlessly and spontaneously accomplish the well-being of others.

The phrase 'A precious human rebirth is difficult to find' covers three points. Firstly, leisure and endowments are difficult to find; not all humans enjoy all eighteen. Secondly, such a human life is very rare because it is difficult to assemble the causes necessary for such a rebirth. Finally, such a human life can be very meaningful because, with the support of conducive conditions, we can achieve consummate happiness and eliminate suffering for ourselves and others. These are just a few points to reflect on.

Contemplating the certainty of death

The phrase 'there's not much time in this life' also covers three points. Even though a human life with leisure and endowments is difficult to find, and despite the fact that it is very meaningful, we still make plans assuming we will live for a long time to come. We might think that there will always be time to take advantage of this life. But when we consider the implications of the statement, 'there's not much time in this life', we see that things might not turn out as we expect. We can never know with certainty whether we will have time to accomplish our long-term plans.

We think first about how death is certain and second how the time of death is uncertain. Though we know this is so, we hope that we will be the exception — that we will not have to die. But this is impossible, for death is certain. Even if we recognise that death is certain, we might still believe that we will live a long time yet. And we think that, as death is a long way off, we will be able to complete our plans. But this is not so, for the time of our death is not established with any certainty. We do not know how much longer we have to live — the time of death is uncertain.

Death is certain and the time of death is uncertain. Together these two are dangerous. It is illogical to assume that we will live as long as we plan for, and inappropriate to act as if that were so. The fact that we have this precious and rare human life does not mean we will also have time to take advantage of it. In light of the certainty of death and the uncertainty of its time, we must take advantage of this rare and meaningful opportunity right now.

Renunciation: the intention to definitively emerge

Contemplating the certainty of death and the uncertainty of the time of death is important, not just in terms of the Dharma but also from a worldly perspective. In Dharma terms, contemplation of these two points is important; the Dharma is essentially a system of skilful means that facilitates the elimination of suffering. If death is certain and the time of death uncertain, we must employ these methods now, from this moment forwards, for we may not have the chance later.

From a worldly perspective it is important to live an honourable life; to be close to others, and to be a good person. If you have a family, it is important that you contribute to the happiness of your family and that you don't spend all your time quarrelling with them. If you recognise the fact that death is a certainty and are aware that there is no certainty about when it will happen, you will conduct your affairs in a different way. You will not spend all of your time quarrelling, disagreeing or being unhappy with your family. You won't nurse grudges but instead will try to resolve any conflicts quickly. You do not want to die regretting a family life filled with strife and unhappiness, or that you never made up with someone.

Being aware of these points is important: it strongly encourages us to be responsible and contribute to our own happiness rather than spend all of our time in disagreements.

It is a great loss and a great pity for someone to live in cyclic existence and experience nothing but suffering. As long as we are not free of cyclic existence, we might as well live happily and enjoy ourselves.

No reason or logic is necessary to prove that death is certain and the time of death is uncertain because we clearly see that this is the case. So the fault does not lie in a lack of understanding, but in a failure to remember and be mindful of these points. When we forget about this we have less impetus to realise the value of this life of leisures and endowments. We forget the necessity and the urgency of seizing this opportunity. It is difficult for young children to understand the benefits of recollecting death; but once we reach a certain age we should begin to appreciate the many benefits that come from being mindful of these points and the many shortcomings of failing to do so.

Lastly, 'there's not much time in this life' indicates that at the time of death nothing but our spiritual practice is of benefit. Perhaps it is helpful to consider the various reasons for this.

There are four things that must be considered. At the time of death, material possessions and wealth cannot save us. Our friends, relatives and those we love cannot save us. Nor is our body of any benefit, because the body cannot stop the process of dying; we must leave the body behind. None of these things — material possessions and wealth; friends, relatives or loved ones; our body — can turn back death, and all of them must be left behind. Therefore, they are of no use at the time of death. Only the mind and its potentials continues past death and the only thing beneficial at that time is our spiritual practice — the preparations we have undertaken for this moment and the positive seeds these have left.

The mind's potential continues along with the mind. The capacities that were instilled in the mind before death are carried with the mind into subsequent lives. These capacities or potentials may be dharmic or non-dharmic. States of mind compatible with the Dharma and the results we derive from cultivating those are 'dharmic capacities'. These will all lead to happiness in the future, whereas non-dharmic states of mind — anger, pride, jealousy and the other disturbing emotions — will produce only suffering in the future.

In brief, both mind and the potentials it holds continue beyond death. Whether the future rebirth is pleasant or unpleasant depends on the potentials of mind. The more we accustom ourselves to positive states of mind compatible with Dharma before we die, the more we stand to gain at death and beyond. Imbuing the mind with positive potentials leads to future happiness. These are the reasons that at the time of death nothing but our spiritual practice is of benefit.

The basic assumption here is that we will take another

rebirth. If there are future lives beyond this one, it is meaningful to discuss what happens after death. Thus it is important to give some thought to whether we will take rebirth after death. If there is a continuity of life and we are bound to be reborn, we might be in danger! What type of rebirth will we take? Some people might find themselves unable to prepare for future lives, in which case we best hope that there will be no future rebirths! We must prepare for the future right now.

I have studied Buddhism with some objectivity for many years now. In these years, I have seen that there are many valid reasons that prove we have taken rebirth in the past and will do so in the future. I have not encountered any valid reasons that conclusively prove that this is not the case. In fact, the more deeply I study, the clearer it becomes that there must be past and future rebirths. If you too investigate these questions objectively, you might also find evidence to support this. And even if you are unsure, there is no harm in living your life assuming that mind continues beyond death. It can spur you on to living a more positive life so that whatever happens after death, at least you will be happier in this life!

The text states that we must familiarise our mind with six points so that we may reverse the infatuation we have with this lifetime and our attachment to its pleasures:

- A precious human life in which we enjoy the eighteen leisures and endowments is difficult to find.

Renunciation: the intention to definitively emerge

- The causes of a precious human life are difficult to assemble and it is therefore rare.
- A precious human life can be very meaningful.
- Death is certain.
- The time of death is uncertain.
- At the time of death nothing but our spiritual practice is of benefit.

By familiarising ourselves with these points through reflection and meditation, we can reverse the tendency to strive solely for the happiness and pleasures of this life. Being mindful of these six points helps us to do so.

Meditating on these points

It is important to meditate upon these points. By doing so, we become familiar with these attitudes, but also develop certain doubts. Right now you may not have a lot of questions, but if you spend some time thinking about these six points you begin to ask, 'How can that be? What are the implications of this?' Contrary as it may seem, generating doubt is a good way to develop wisdom because it gives you the opportunity to question and further clarify particular points.

Is renunciation necessary? Is it necessary to have the intention to definitively emerge from cyclic existence? Without it we do not fully seek liberation. Why not? Because we would still be attached to the pleasures of samsara. What is the happiness of liberation? It is the happiness that is free of suffering. Samsaric happiness is infused with suffering. What is the difference between these two? Happiness infused with suffering is temporary, brief and unreliable. Why? Because it depends in part on the causes of suffering. As long as we have not abandoned suffering and its causes, any happiness we experience will be samsaric happiness — brief, unreliable and temporary. The happiness of liberation doesn't rely at all on the causes of suffering. It is therefore free of suffering; it is reliable, lasting and satisfying.

Eight mundane concerns

Lama Tsongkhapa says that reflecting on the rarity of a precious human rebirth, the inevitability of death and the unpredictability of its onset will help to stem infatuation with this life. To stem infatuation with this life, we must develop renunciation — the positive wish to definitively emerge from cyclic existence.

In addition, we must overcome the eight mundane concerns. These keep us bound up in samsaric pursuits and the limited pleasures related to those. The noble Nagarjuna introduces the eight mundane concerns in his text *A Letter to a Friend*:

> You who know the world and its ways! Gain and not gain,
> Pleasure and displeasure, pleasing statements and displeasing ones,

Renunciation: the intention to definitively emerge

> *Praise and abuse, are the eight mundane concerns.*
> *Keep a level head and do not concern yourself with them!* [1]

To be attached to gain is one mundane concern; another is to be attached to reputation. If we cannot maintain a level head about such things we are easily excited by financial gain and flattering words, and easily upset by loss and rumour. If we are not shown the respect we feel we deserve, we become upset. We get upset because we are attached to our reputation. The same is true in terms of loss. If we are greatly attached to financial gain, we feel emotionally deflated when we fail to acquire the expected gain.

Our attachment to such mundane concerns leads to anger and discouragement when our wishes are not met and an exaggerated confidence when they are. In short, the eight mundane concerns disrupt our mind's stability and put us on an emotional roller-coaster. With a level head towards our reputation and displays of respect we will be unfaltering in all circumstances, regardless of the respect, or lack of it, we are shown.

It is the same with any of the other mundane concerns. Take pleasure and displeasure for example. We are so attached to pleasure that when we don't experience the pleasure we seek we become upset and let down. As long as we are attached to pleasure, even the slightest sufferings will be unbearable.

At the same time, we will never be satisfied with the amount of pleasure we experience.

Thinking only of pleasure and being completely averse to suffering of any kind, we will find that no pleasure is wholly satisfying and all sufferings are unbearable. This will remain true as long as we are attached to samsaric pleasures. This mindset causes us to bounce between exhilaration and depression. If we were not so attached to pleasure, minor sufferings would not be unbearable and our appetite for pleasure not so insatiable.

With a level head and a balanced attitude towards pleasure and suffering we are not so subject to the emotional extremes of overexcitement and depression. Small pleasures and sufferings are not exaggerated: the greater the exaggeration the greater the fall, the deeper the disappointment when pleasure dissipates and suffering sets in.

We all want to be happy and no one wants to suffer. There is nothing wrong with this. We should try to stop suffering before it manifests, by avoiding the actions that cause it and by looking after our health, both physical and mental. However, once suffering manifests, as it inevitably does, it is best to accept it. We will only make things worse if, at that point, we continue in our desire not to suffer at all. It does no good to reject suffering if suffering has already manifested.

Maintaining a level head is important. If we cannot

Renunciation: the intention to definitively emerge

maintain stability of mind, our experience of happiness and any subsequent sufferings become an exaggerated roller-coaster of emotional ups and downs. Without attachment to happiness and suffering we can maintain a level head. We can enjoy pleasure and happiness, for there is nothing wrong with this. But exaggeration is dangerous; it sets us up for a fall.

The eight mundane concerns are presented in four sets of two each. We have just covered 'gain and no gain' and 'pleasure and displeasure'. We have also mentioned reputation. The third set relates to the way we like things to be expressed in a pleasant manner. We do not like things that are expressed in unpleasant ways even if they are helpful.

We should try not to be attached to the things people say to us, even though this is our tendency. Though we tend to be upset by the unpleasant things that are said to us we do not need to be. To apply these instructions, we must feel that there is no difference between pleasing and displeasing words. Then we can be level-headed about what others say to us. But don't think this means that you can say whatever you like, however you like, to others! The teachings on mind-training emphasise the importance of communicating with others in a respectful way. We should not look down on others. So although we must not be too concerned with how others express themselves to us, we must be careful with the way we express ourselves to others!

Praise does not cause our qualities to increase; criticism and abuse does not make them diminish. We are neither improved nor diminished by what people say about us. We have a particular nature and the praise or scorn others heap on us will not in itself change that.

We should think of praise and abuse as being like echoes. If you yell in an empty canyon, the sound of your voice returns to you. If you shout abuse or praise, it simply bounces off the canyon walls and returns to you without helping or harming you. The same is true for the words of others: they do not improve or diminish you in any way, so think of them as like an echo.

Once we begin to think about how we are affected by these mundane concerns, we quickly see how we are attached to the pleasures of samsara. When we look at our reactions to these eight different occurrences, we see how attached to gain, pleasure, pleasing statements and praise we are and how averse to loss, suffering, displeasing statements and criticism we are.

As long as we are wrapped up in these mundane concerns, our practice of Dharma will not develop properly. While we pursue gain and praise and so on, our efforts will only improve our worldly status and increase our mundane concerns. This means our activities will not act as causes for liberation and so will not lead to its stable and satisfying happiness.

The eight mundane concerns hinder our spiritual practice, inflame our infatuation with this life and stop us from developing the intention to definitively emerge from cyclic existence.

The rest of the fourth verse reads:

> *If you reflect again and again on the unfailing effects of action,*
> *And the sufferings of samsara, infatuation with future lives*
>   *will also stop.*

We can stop our infatuation with future lives and our desire for pleasures from them by reflecting again and again on the sufferings of cyclic existence. A person who believes in rebirth can easily become attached to what the future holds, just as we are attached to this life. Some might become infatuated with the idea of enjoying great wealth, and seek to be reborn to rich parents. It is okay to consider what type of circumstances would be conducive in future lives. But if our actions are only motivated by the desire for future samsaric happiness, we are still attached to samsaric pleasures and will not escape from the cycle of conditioned existence. As long as we are oriented towards samsaric states — now or in the future — our efforts will not lead to liberation.

The effects of actions are 'unfailing' in that they do not deceive. That is, positive actions cause positive effects; negative actions cause negative effects. Though there are many types of causes, here we are talking about substantial causes. A substantial cause is the cause without which the effect could not arise. A substantial cause changes to become the effect. A positive substantial cause will always lead to a positive effect; a negative substantial cause will always result in a negative effect. For instance, if you beat gold into the shape of a cup it will be a golden cup. If you mould clay into a cup it will be a clay cup. The material with which you make the cup is the substantial cause. If gold is the material you are working with, the final product will not be made of clay. This illustrates the 'unfailing' nature of actions and their effects.

Cause and effect as it operates internally is called 'karma and its effects'. The Sanskrit word *karma* means 'action'. Actions cause certain effects. Think about it: what are the effects of positive action? What types of events and experiences in this life are caused by positive actions? What about in future rebirths? It is difficult to fully understand the unfailing effect of actions; yet to understand it better, we should think about the effects certain actions have. Begin by thinking about negative actions. What would happen to us in this life if we were to kill someone? What if we were to steal? What are the effects of sexual misconduct like infidelity?

Many people think 'karma' is a Buddhist or Hindu notion. They think, 'Since I am not a Buddhist it does not affect me.' But karma means action; everyone acts and everyone experiences the effects of their actions. When Lama Tsongkhapa encourages us to respect the unfailing effects of actions, he encourages us to develop confidence that actions of a certain type cause effects of a certain type. In this respect, actions are unfailing or non-deceptive. You can't trick a positive cause into becoming a negative result. This confidence is not blind faith; such conviction arises after you have investigated the way things are and seen the accuracy of it.

There are four points to reflect on in relation to actions and their effects. These four ought to help us understand and deepen our meditation on actions and their effects:
- Actions are definite.
- Actions increase.
- We do not encounter the effects of actions that we have not performed.
- The effects of actions do not go to waste.

Since effects arise from causes of a similar type, either positive or negative actions are said to be definite. Positive causes give rise to positive effects and negative effects arise from negative causes. When a seed is planted in a garden a certain type of plant sprouts up. If the seed is from a chilli, the plant's fruit will not be sweet; if the seed is from a medicinal plant, the plant will not be a poisonous one.

Karma, or action, is really cause and effect operating internally. Just as we can see that positive causes lead to positive effect in the external environment, we can infer the same of internal cause and effect. If the effects of external events are definite, there is no reason to think the internal effects of actions are not.

We all have a basic understanding of cause and effect. We know that killing, stealing, infidelity and speaking harsh or untrue words are negative actions that have negative effects. Understanding these general principles helps us understand the more subtle workings of cause and effect.

We can then guide ourselves towards positive actions and away from negative ones. In fact, this naturally happens once we see that future fruits resemble present actions. From understanding comes conviction and confidence; and from these, good and helpful advice from within.

Since the effect of an action is greater than the action itself, actions are said to increase. A single small action may result in enormous suffering lasting a long time. This is also true in the outside world. A single apple seed can produce an apple tree and a bountiful harvest year after year. Knowing this, we will avoid even minor negative actions and not overlook positive acts that seem insignificant.

Disturbing emotions

Disturbing emotions are a cause of suffering. Freedom from suffering occurs when we abandon them and their seeds. But

Renunciation: the intention to definitively emerge

to attain such liberation we must have a strong wish to abandon the causes of suffering. This fierce intention to emerge from suffering into liberation is renunciation. Our attachment to the pleasures of cyclic existence prevents us from developing such a strong wish for liberation.

Buddhism's fundamental principle is that the main causes for suffering can be found in our own minds, not in the world around us. Initially we might object to this idea, saying, 'I suffer because so and so treated me poorly and said a hurtful thing. That person is the cause of my suffering.' Yet if we look more closely we find that this is not the case; there is a flaw in the logic. What if that person said something nasty to a rock? Would the rock experience suffering?

You may be thinking, 'It's just a rock; it doesn't have any feelings. How could it experience suffering?' I welcome this questioning because it gives us an opportunity to examine the truth of the example. In fact, it only proves the point. The very same external conditions create suffering in a person but not in a rock, so how could those conditions be the cause of suffering? If they were really a cause for suffering they ought to create suffering in everything they encounter, animate or inanimate. But suffering does not occur without a cause and that cause cannot be found in external things. It is as true for rocks as it is for people and other life forms.

Take someone who has a superbly developed practice

of patience, for example. This type of person revels in the opportunity to practise patience, so he or she is delighted when another person is hostile towards him or her. Such a person derives great joy from practising patience and such difficulties are required to really practise it. So keen on patience, the person has virtually no cause to suffer. Hence, nasty words and hostile acts do not upset them.

Our reaction to nasty words is a good gauge of our patience. How well do we respond in such situations? When we have tasted the Dharma, we enjoy cultivating good qualities like patience. A person who genuinely enjoys giving will be overjoyed when another asks them for something, like money. This person would happily give it, thinking, 'Great, another opportunity to practise generosity. Here my friend, take this.'

A penny-pinching person, on the other hand, is troubled by such a request. Unable to give easily, he or she might think, 'Why do you have to ask me? I wish you hadn't asked me. I wish you'd get lost.' The very same request brings one person joy and another person turmoil. A person who enjoys putting virtues into practice will delight at the opportunity to do so. Others will be troubled by such circumstances. The difference between these two is readily apparent.

We do not encounter the effects of actions that we have not performed. It is easier to accept suffering if we under-

Renunciation: the intention to definitively emerge

stand that the cause of our present suffering comes from actions we ourselves have done in the past. Suffering in the present is a sign that we have made others suffer in the past. Harmful actions motivated by ill will leave seeds behind in the mind. These seeds carry the potential for suffering. Later, certain conditions activate the seed, awakening the potential for suffering. If we had not harmed another, the potential for suffering would not exist in our minds. If we apply a counter-force, namely goodwill, to past acts of ill will, we can render those seeds incapable of producing an effect. In other words, we can remove the potential for suffering by cultivating goodwill.

Positive actions and Dharma practice sow the seeds for free and fortunate human rebirths in the future, but we have still committed many negative actions in the past and these need to be purified. In countless former lives, we have certainly sown the seeds for unfortunate rebirths. Knowing that actions are definite — good causes lead to good effects and bad causes lead to bad effects — and that we do not encounter the effects of actions that we have not performed, we will recognise the precariousness of our situation. Though we act properly now, there is still the danger that past actions will propel us into negative states in the future; for actions, once performed, do not go to waste.

How is it that performed actions do not just disappear

without a trace? Is it correct to say that the intention to act precedes the act itself? Before a person murders another, they develop the intention to kill. Initially, the intention 'I will kill them' leaves behind a certain potential or latent propensity in the mind. Later, the mind is active while the act is committed. Although killing is a physical act, the mind directs and is involved with the physical act. The act is completed when the person dies, at which point a seed of complete action is placed in mind. This seed carries a potential and propensity commensurate with the strength of the intention and the act.

Actions are stored in the mind as seeds. Mind is thus the container in which karmic seeds are carried from life to life. Since the container is never destroyed, its contents will never simply go to waste. Seeds may come to fruition, or be destroyed in one of a few ways. Certain virtuous seeds, if left unprotected, can be destroyed by anger. Non-virtuous seeds can be destroyed by the four antidotal powers: developing regret about what was done; resolving not to do it again; relying on a support like the Buddha, Dharma and Sangha Jewels: and applying an antidote like loving-kindness or compassion.

As actions leave seeds in the form of mental propensities, we must use the mind itself to rid ourselves of them. Applying the four antidotal powers renders these seeds incapable

Renunciation: the intention to definitively emerge

of producing an unpleasant effect. The karmic potentials of mind will remain as long as none of these things occur. That is why actions, once performed, do not go to waste.

Reflecting on these points helps us to overcome our attachment to the pleasures of future lives. Striving for happiness in future lives is a waste of the virtue we have worked so hard to accumulate. The motivation we bring to each virtuous act limits or extends its reach. If we do not think, 'May this be a cause for liberation,' our actions will not act as causes for liberation. If we strive solely for higher status rebirths, our virtues cannot act as causes for anything more than that. Limiting the scope of our actions limits the scope of their effects, whereas expanding the scope of our actions does not limit their effects. If we are motivated by the thought, 'May this be a cause for liberation,' our virtues can bring both liberation *and* higher status rebirths as a human, to say nothing of happiness here and beyond. There are great benefits from performing virtue with the motivation to attain the happiness of liberation.

We shortchange ourselves and diminish the impact of virtue with short-sighted motivations, for the same virtue under the influence of a greater motivation, like the wish to attain liberation, will accomplish lesser goals as a by-product.

Once we see that samsaric pleasure is unreliable, we can understand that higher status states in cyclic existence will not satisfy us in the future either. Reflecting on this will help us to overcome attachment to future happinesses.

Reflecting on each of these four points encourages a particular way of thinking:

- Thinking about how actions are definite encourages us to avoid negative actions.
- Thinking about how actions increase encourages us to refrain from even minor unskilful acts that might entail negative actions and consequences.
- Thinking about how we do not encounter the effect of actions we have not done encourages us to see that the seed for all experiences, pleasant or unpleasant, comes from within. The source of happiness, and of suffering, lies within the mind, not external things. It is not as if these experiences arise without rhyme or reason.
- Thinking about how an action, once performed, does not go to waste encourages us to acknowledge and purify our negative actions with the four antidotal powers. Unless negative karmic potentials are confessed and purified they will result in unwanted suffering. When we purify negative seeds, we render them unable to produce an unpleasant effect.

Let's reverse this process and think about these four points as they apply to liberation. Suppose we decide to abandon the disturbing emotions, which are causes of suffering, in order to attain liberation:

Renunciation: the intention to definitively emerge

- Understanding that actions are definite, we will gather the causes for liberation. Since certain actions definitely lead to certain effects, the only way to get positive results is to accumulate positive causes.
- Understanding that actions increase, we will not dismiss minor virtues. Knowing that the effects of an action are greater than the act itself, we try to act positively, aware that even seemingly small acts can have huge results.
- Knowing that we do not encounter the effect of actions we have not done encourages us to gather the causes for liberation. The attainment of liberation does not happen on its own; it relies upon positive causes *and* the motivation to attain it. Simply praying to the Three Jewels is not enough. We cannot attain our goal through prayer alone; we must also gather the causes for it.
- Understanding that actions, once accumulated, do not go to waste encourages us to protect our roots of virtue from anger, as explained in Chapter 7. Just as confession and purification can purify negative seeds, anger can wipe out a positive seed's ability to produce pleasant effects. Unless exhausted or destroyed by anger, positive seeds remain, without going to waste, in the mind.

The main reason we reflect on actions and their effects is to overcome our attachment to the happiness of future lives. Yet it can also help us overcome our attachment to the pleasures of this life. If we are no longer attached to samsaric pleasures, we will stop our single-minded pursuit of them. This change in attitude allows us to reorient ourselves towards liberation so our actions act as causes for it. As long as we strive solely for the happinesses of cyclic existence, our positive actions will not become causes for liberation.

These points were made in the third verse:

> *Without pure renunciation there is no way to stop chasing after Pleasurable things within the ocean of samsara.*

The ocean of samsara is the ocean of conditioned existence. In brief, this verse states that we cannot become free from cyclic existence if we do not develop the intention to definitively emerge from it. Our attachment to its pleasures prevents us from developing a strong wish to attain the happiness of liberation.

The root of all of our problems can be traced back to the five disturbing emotions. Ignorance is the main one, which we will leave aside for now. Anger, attachment, pride and envy are the remaining four. These four disturbing emotions develop from our constantly chasing the pleasures of samsara. At the same time, our pursuit of them depends on the disturbing emotions themselves. It's quite obvious; in striving for samsaric pleasures we become attached to them. Attached

Renunciation: the intention to definitively emerge

to the pleasures of samsara we get angry when we can't have them. We become angry at and envious of whatever comes between ourselves and pleasure. Our pride is threatened and we feel anger towards those who stand in the way of our happiness. There is a reciprocal relationship between our pursuit of samsaric pleasure and the disturbing emotions. Though this pursuit is propelled by the disturbing emotions, the pursuit itself exacerbates and inflames them.

The fifth verse reads:

> *When, through familiarity, the wish for the highest pleasures*
>   *of samsara*
> *Does not arise for even a single moment*
> *And all the time, day and night, you aim for liberation,*
> *Renunciation has truly been born.*

Disturbing emotions are causes of suffering. Liberation is the abandonment of disturbing emotions and their causes. A very strong intention to abandon the causes of suffering is required to attain liberation. Renunciation sees the drawbacks of cyclic existence and has a fierce intention to attain liberation. Attachment to and pursuit of the pleasures of samsara prevent us from developing a fierce intention to seek and attain liberation.

How do we know that samsaric pleasures are no longer

our main aim? If we do not wish for them, not even for a moment, they are no longer our chief pursuit. And further, when day and night we think of achieving freedom, at that point we have developed renunciation, the intention to definitively emerge.

Reflecting on the sufferings of samsara strengthens and supports the intention to definitively emerge. Some forms of suffering are universal, present in all forms of cyclic existence. There are other types of suffering that are characteristic of the negative or unfortunate rebirths. We must consider why we experience suffering and recognise the limitations and drawbacks of samsaric states.

Again, how does the pursuit of samsaric pleasures lead to suffering? Pursuing samsaric pleasures feeds disturbing emotions, like anger, attachment and envy. Disturbing emotions in turn lead us to speak, act and think in certain ways. Such actions of body, speech and mind place karmic seeds in the mind — seeds that later ripen into suffering.

Perhaps this is a bit difficult to understand. Does the pursuit of samsaric pleasures really result in suffering? Let's look at an example. While bound by disturbing emotions, our enjoyment of food is a samsaric pleasure. Attached to the pleasure that comes with a nice meal, a person who loves seafood catches a fish and in the process kills it. The pursuit of pleasure leads to an act of killing.

Renunciation: the intention to definitively emerge

Seeking pleasure, a person might have an affair with a married person; yet this is sexual misconduct and a non-virtue. The person's pursuit of pleasure leads them to a non-virtue. Or perhaps we lash out at another person because they obstruct our pursuit of pleasure. Our single-minded pursuit leads us to ill will and the use of harsh words. Killing, sexual misconduct, harsh speech and ill will are all products of our single-minded pursuit of samsaric pleasures.

Dharma practice should be aimed at developing antidotes and abandoning disturbing emotions. If it is, our positive qualities will increase and negative states of mind will diminish. In practising the Dharma, we try to reduce disturbing emotions while nurturing the positive qualities of wisdom, loving kindness and compassion, and so on.

As Dharma practitioners we pray, and although it is a good thing to do, in itself it is not enough. In the worst cases a person places all of their hopes in prayer without doing anything to support those prayers. This is very unfortunate and not very beneficial.

Suppose I like apples and want some in my garden. It would be silly to pray every day for apples to grow in my garden if I don't have an apple tree and haven't even planted a seed for one! How can you have apples with no tree, or a tree with no seed? Just so, it is impossible to experience the effect of things we have no cause for. So prayers are good, but they need to be supplemented by actions and causes. We need to transform our minds, for that is the support prayers require to be helpful and effective.

6

Bodhicitta:
the mind of enlightenment

The mind of enlightenment, or bodhicitta, is the heart of the Great Vehicle's path. In cultivating the mind of enlightenment, the qualities of wisdom and compassion increase like a waxing moon, so that we are of greater benefit to others. The mind of enlightenment has two aspects: ultimate and relative. The relative mind of enlightenment is a mind that seeks buddhahood for the sake of all sentient beings. The ultimate mind of enlightenment is qualified by that same mind, but, in addition, perceptually realises emptiness. This chapter explores the different facets of the mind of enlightenment and discusses how we can develop it to its utmost potential. In this chapter we discuss verses 6 to 8 of *The Three Principal Aspects of the Path*.

Verses 6 to 8 of
The Three Principal Aspects of the Path

Why we need to develop bodhicitta

6   *Unless it's driven by pure bodhicitta,*
Renunciation will never become a cause
For the perfect happiness of highest enlightenment.
Therefore intelligent beings cultivate supreme bodhicitta.

The way to develop bodhicitta

7   *Carried away by the torrents of four fierce rivers;*
Bound by tight fetters of karma, difficult to undo;
Caught up in the iron net of self-grasping;
Completely enveloped by the pitch-black darkness of ignorance.

8   *In a never-ending cycle, in birth after birth,*
They're tormented without a break by the three types of suffering;
By thinking about the plight of mother sentient beings
In circumstances like these, develop the supreme mind.

> *A mind of enlightenment knows no prejudice or favouritism, for it is interested in the welfare of all beings equally. It is a supremely wholesome mind and can overcome all negativities. It is a courageous mind that does not turn away from the hardships of helping others. It is the gateway to the Mahayana paths.*

Renunciation alone does not lead to our main goal, which is buddhahood. Seeing the shortcomings of samsara, renunciation remains unattached to them and strives for the pleasures of liberation. You need renunciation to develop a mind of enlightenment but you cannot develop consummate wisdom, compassion and ability simply through renunciation alone. With time, a mind of enlightenment strengthens our intention to definitively emerge so the two work in tandem. Lama Tsongkhapa said that thinking about suffering in relation to oneself and finding it unbearable is renunciation, and thinking about suffering in relation to others and finding that unbearable is compassion. If the thought of your own suffering does not strike you as intolerable, how can you be moved by the thought that others suffer?

What is bodhicitta?
Verse six reads:

> *Unless it's driven by pure bodhicitta,*
> *Renunciation will never become a cause*
> *For the perfect happiness of highest enlightenment.*
> *Therefore intelligent beings cultivate supreme bodhicitta.*

Firstly, it is important to understand what bodhicitta is. Bodhicitta, or a mind of enlightenment, is a mind with two aspirations: a causal and an assisting aspiration. The causal aspiration is an aspiration that strives for the sake of others. It is a wish to free sentient beings from their suffering through our own actions. The assisting aspiration is an aspiration that strives for the sake of enlightenment. It is a wish to attain buddhahood in order to accomplish the first aspiration. Together these two form the thought, 'May I attain buddhahood so that I can free all sentient beings from suffering.' The mind of enlightenment itself is a mind, while the two aspirations are mental events that accompany the mind.

When a person develops the strong wish to free others from suffering, that person might wonder if he or she has the ability to do so. Wanting to free others but limited in ability, the person aspires to develop their wisdom, compassion and ability. The causal aspiration is based on the wish to implement more effectively the assisting aspiration. The mind of enlightenment develops as the second aspiration is established: the two occur simultaneously. As a cause, the causal aspiration is a necessary prerequisite for a mind of enlightenment. As the assisting aspiration develops, the mind comes to possess both aspirations and thus becomes a mind of enlightenment.

The aspiration to assume personal responsibility for the welfare of all sentient beings is the highest intention. This highest intention precedes bodhicitta and is itself preceded by great compassion. Often loving-kindness will come before great compassion, but this is not always the case. Before we develop either loving-kindness or great compassion we must develop the type of empathy that finds all sentient beings appealing and feels drawn to them. Without this, neither great compassion nor the highest intention is possible, let alone a mind of enlightenment.

Developing a mind drawn to others

There are two techniques used to develop an empathetic mind drawn to all sentient beings:
- The first is to develop the recognition that all sentient beings have been our mother, remembering their kindness and then wishing to repay that kindness. These are the

first three steps in the 'sevenfold instructions on cause and effect', which is explained later in this chapter.
- The second technique involves reflecting on the shortcomings of cherishing oneself to the exclusion of others and the benefits of cherishing others before self. This technique is called 'equalising and exchanging self for others'.

Great compassion must come before a mind of enlightenment; we must feel drawn to others before we develop great compassion for them. Either of these two techniques can be used to achieve this.

What is the purpose in recognising that all sentient beings have been our mother? To establish a sense of closeness, which makes them more appealing to us so that we feel drawn to them. Traditionally, this type of attitude is illustrated by the love between a mother and her only beloved child. To develop empathetic loving-kindness and great compassion we must be drawn to all sentient beings, as a mother is to her sole and dear child and vice versa.

Once we feel close to others and recognise that they have been kind to us, it is natural to feel drawn to them. But not everyone feels that his or her mother has been so kind. Our mother nurtured us for nine months while we were in her womb, suckled us at her breast and cared for us in our early years. Often we forget those years of kindness because of quarrels we had as teenagers or mistakes that one or the other has made since. Although these things make us forget the kindness, they do not nullify it. Furthermore, there is no sentient being who has not been our mother at one point in the past. We have taken rebirth many times without beginning, so many times that each being has had the chance to be our mother. Reflecting on the kindness of the mother and recognising that all sentient beings have acted as our mother can help us to develop a mind drawn to others.

It is important that our empathy be based on equanimity. Without equanimity, we will be biased and partial and our attitude towards friend, foe and stranger will not be balanced. Equanimity helps us overcome partial feelings of closeness and distance so that our empathy embraces all.

Reverse order of generating a mind of enlightenment

A mind of enlightenment arises after developing equanimity, empathy, loving-kindness, compassion and the highest intention. This is the 'forward order' by which the mind of enlightenment arises. From time to time we should also meditate on this process in reverse, beginning with the mind of enlightenment.

By thinking about the two aspirations of the mind of enlightenment we come to see how it cannot arise without the highest intention. To take personal responsibility for relieving others of suffering, we must have great compassion. The wish that others be free of suffering comes from the empathy that feels drawn to others. To feel drawn to them and find all sentient beings appealing, we must be aware of their kindness to us. That awareness can be gained through either of the two techniques on pages 181 and 192. For empathy and concern to extend towards all, it must be founded upon equanimity.

A fully fledged mind of enlightenment must be based on equanimity. Reflecting on the 'reverse order' helps us to appreciate that. We can begin meditating on the forward order once we are familiar with equanimity. Alternating between the forward and reverse orders and repeating them over and over again is like exercising the mind. Our minds become more flexible and it becomes easier and easier. Eventually a new understanding begins to form with time and patience.

To attain the pure state of buddhahood we must have compassion. To attain the pure state we must have a pure mind. A pure mind is not driven by malicious self-interest, but in striving for complete enlightenment we must still fulfil our own aims as well as the aims of others. Bodhisattvas, much less buddhas, do not cherish themselves over others. In cultivating a mind of enlightenment, we must exchange our self-cherishing tendencies for a mind that cherishes others.

Developing renunciation — the intention to definitively emerge — spurs us on towards liberation since in developing it we recognise how pervasive our suffering is. Compassion develops when this recognition extends to other sentient beings as well. Knowing how intolerable our own suffering is, we want to be free from it. Knowing how intolerable others' suffering is, we want them to be free from it.

Compassion helps us develop the first of the mind of enlightenment's two aspirations — the wish to free all sentient beings from suffering. That, together with renunciation, helps us develop the second — the wish to achieve buddhahood so that we can better accomplish the first. Thus we cannot develop a mind of enlightenment, nor can we become buddhas, by cherishing ourselves alone.

What is compassion?

Compassion is the simple wish that someone else be free of suffering. It is a very general term. A person may have compassion for humans but not for animals, or for animals but not for humans. Compassion can be partial; it does not necessarily extend to all. But this is mere compassion, not great compassion. The prerequisite for the mind of enlightenment is great, not mere, compassion. Great compassion extends towards all sentient beings and is based on equanimity.

We may see a person or animal suffer and wish that it did not suffer. That alone does not make great compassion. In recognising that one being suffers, we must recognise that

Bodhicitta: the mind of enlightenment

there are others who are similarly tormented. The suffering we witness is an illustration of that which affects others as well, and great compassion takes this into account. Great compassion wants all sentient beings who are tormented by suffering to be free from suffering and its causes. So in seeing one being suffer, we call to mind others who suffer and wish that they were all free of suffering.

To attain buddhahood we must *want* to attain buddhahood. The desire for buddhahood is based on the recognition that, at present, we are limited in our ability to help others; yet if we developed consummate wisdom, compassion and ability, things would be different. In short, the desire is based on the highest intention of compassion and an appreciation of buddhahood's qualities.

Buddhahood is a state of consummate wisdom, compassion and ability. A mind of enlightenment wants to attain that state to free others from suffering. How then can we develop a mind of enlightenment without compassion? How can you attain a state of consummate compassion without cherishing others? How can you attain buddhahood without a mind that understands and seeks it?

Before we have consummate compassion we must have great compassion. For great compassion we must be drawn to all sentient beings, and for that we need an equanimity that quells attachment, hostility and indifference.

Developing equanimity

As it stands, we are attached to those we feel close to, hostile to those we dislike and indifferent to those in between. To develop equanimity means to stop our attachment to friends, hostility to adversaries and indifference to strangers and replace them with a balanced and even mind. Once that is accomplished we substitute compassion for attachment, loving-kindness for hostility and a cherishing mind for indifference.

Think about all the problems caused by attachment, hostility and indifference. Our attachment exaggerates the appeal of people and things and prevents us from seeing their faults. Think of what happens when our attachment diminishes and we see a person as he or she really is, not in the glorified way we were captivated by. Our hostility makes us say and do nasty things and our indifference hardens us to the plight of others so we no longer care if our pleasure comes at their expense. Now imagine how pleasant and happy we would be if we replaced these with compassion, loving-kindness and a mind that cherishes others. How many problems would we prevent?

Thinking about these points helps us to develop the genuine feeling that we must generate a mind of enlightenment and attain buddhahood. Without equanimity, empathy, loving-kindness, compassion and the highest intention we cannot develop a mind of enlightenment. And if even a single sentient being is excluded from our compassion we cannot develop great compassion, to say nothing of consummate compassion.

As we have seen, renunciation — the intention to definitively emerge — alone is not enough to attain buddhahood, the highest and most perfect type of happiness. For that we need a mind of enlightenment.

The most excellent bliss is experienced only in buddhahood. Even the bliss of mere liberation, which is peaceful, unchanging, and unmarked by suffering, pales in comparison. Why? Though a person abandons disturbing emotions and their seeds in attaining liberation, he or she is still bound by the imprints and mistaken appearances of ignorance — remnants of having grasped at true existence. Such a person has got rid of suffering and its causes and enjoys a peaceful bliss but has not yet attained consummate personal well-being because the imprints and dualistic appearances remain.

A buddha perfects his or her own well-being and is able to accomplish effortlessly the welfare of others. Someone who has removed the emotional obscurations but not the cognitive ones can do neither. Still subject to mistaken appearances and limited in the ability to assist others, such a person does not abide in and cannot establish others in a state of perfect happiness — buddhahood.

This is the difference between an arhat and a buddha. Arhats have abandoned emotional obscurations and attained mere liberation, whereas buddhas have abandoned both emotional and cognitive obscurations and attained unsurpassed supreme liberation. The first can be attained by integrating renunciation and wisdom alone. The second can only be attained if renunciation, wisdom *and* a mind of enlightenment are united in practice.

An intelligent person who has understood this would not be content to settle for mere liberation, but would rather strive for highest complete enlightenment. Knowing that mere liberation is not the ultimate achievement, these intelligent beings arouse a mind of enlightenment so that their practice acts as a cause for buddhahood and the most excellent bliss.

Verses seven and eight read:

> *Carried away by the torrents of four fierce rivers;*
> *Bound by tight fetters of karma, difficult to undo;*
> *Caught up in the iron net of self-grasping;*
> *Completely enveloped by the pitch-black darkness of*
> > *ignorance;*

> *In a never-ending cycle, in birth after birth,*
> *They're tormented without a break by the three types*
> > *of suffering;*
> *By thinking about the plight of mother sentient beings*
> *In circumstances like these, develop the supreme mind.*

Bodhicitta: the mind of enlightenment

These two verses teach us how to develop compassion and a mind of enlightenment by reflecting on the plight of sentient beings. Our minds will only become minds of enlightenment if we gather the causes for it. Two of its main causes are great compassion and great loving-kindness, which arise through thinking about the plight of mother sentient beings.

All sentient beings are ceaselessly tormented by suffering. They are swept along by the strong current of four fierce rivers — desire, conditioned existence, ignorance and wrong views — and suffer as a result. Recognising this, we can develop the wish that they were happy and free of suffering.

Samsaric existence is characterised by five or six features, as the analogy of a person swept powerlessly down the river indicates. Imagine someone trapped within an iron net, their arms and legs bound by ropes, put into a river at night and sent downstream to an uninhabited wilderness. This person cannot get free because their limbs are bound by ropes and they are trapped in an iron net. It is night and there is no one around, so their calls for help go unheeded. Thrown against rocks as they hurtle downstream, the person suffers from many things.

The analogy of the river
The first feature of samsaric existence is symbolised by the 'torrents of four fierce rivers': desire, conditioned existence,

ignorance and wrong views. These symbolise the uncontrolled birth, ageing, illness and death that plague sentient beings controlled by actions and disturbing emotions. We are powerless over these four torrents, which sweep us down the river of cyclic existence.

The second feature is symbolised by the person whose limbs are bound by the tight fetters of karma. This represents how our actions bind us to this body. Contaminated actions bind us to body after body in rebirth after rebirth. Such actions are like strong chains, difficult to undo.

The third feature is symbolised by the fact that the person is caught up in an iron net. The iron net represents self-grasping, a misapprehension of self that traps us. In addition, this misapprehension supports other disturbing emotions, like attachment, anger, pride and envy, which also trap us.

The fourth feature is symbolised by the pitch-black dark of night. The smothering darkness symbolises how we are completely enveloped by ignorance, which keeps us in the dark. The less we know, the greater our ignorance. There are many types of ignorance; here the emphasis is on not knowing the methods that free us from cyclic existence.

Another feature is that we are constantly tormented by suffering of one type or another. Like the person in the analogy who crashes against rocks, shivers in cold water and is surrounded by a thick darkness, samsaric beings are tormented by the suffering of suffering, the suffering of change, and the all-pervasive suffering of conditioning.

The suffering of suffering is what we ordinarily associate with suffering: illness, pain, and so on. We experience the suffering of change when we partake of contaminated pleasures. Initially they are pleasant but eventually they give way to suffering through dissatisfaction, craving, overindulgence, etc. All-pervasive sufferings of conditioning are aggregates that perpetuate contamination and are bound by actions and disturbing emotions. Generally there are five aggregates, the aggregates of body, mind, feeling, discrimination and formation. These are contaminated if they were appropriated through the power of karmic actions and disturbing emotions. We are not always suffering in the ordinary 'suffering of suffering' sense, but our pleasures are short-lived and lead to suffering as long as we are bound by actions and disturbing emotions, and cannot escape the all-pervasive suffering of conditioning.

In summary, the characteristic features of samsara are:
1 We are powerless over birth, ageing, illness and death, which is symbolised by the four rivers that contribute to them.
2 We are bound by karma and disturbing emotions.
3 We are caught up in grasping at the self, which is the root of both actions and disturbing emotions. Self-grasping is not just being ignorant of the nature of the self, but actually

misapprehending it; for instance, wrongly holding it to exist truly or from its own side. This misapprehension underlies our anger, attachment, pride and the rest. We instinctively hold that the self as we see it is true, so that when 'I' am threatened, 'I' become angry with the other person, who we also hold to exist truly.

4 Ignorance is limitless. Ignorance is delusion. We are deluded about the nature of things, which are limitless. We are deluded about how disturbing emotions make us suffer. We are ignorant of how loving-kindness and compassion create happiness. We are deluded about what to adopt and what to discard, what is beneficial and good and what is detrimental and bad. We are ignorant of what methods lead to liberation.

5 Samsara seems to be endless. It would seem that conditioned existence has no beginning and no end. We cannot pinpoint its beginning, even if we search for it. Looking ahead, it is difficult to see an end to suffering, when we will attain liberation.

6 In samsaric states, suffering is uninterrupted. Mother sentient beings are tormented by the three types of suffering without respite. The unbroken continuity of suffering is linked to the seemingly endless cycle of conditioned existence. Looking back we see no break; looking ahead we see none either. Features five and six may be counted as one, leaving us with five features all up.

Types of relationships

Would you feel compassion for a friend thrown into a river where four strong currents toss them about, hurling them against semi-submerged rocks? Imagine it is midnight and only you can see that your friend is drowning, caught up in an iron net, with arms and legs bound by rope. Would you want to help your friend? Would you feel compassion for them?

What if the person in the river was your adversary, someone you didn't like and who constantly criticised you? What if this person acted spitefully towards you and stole what was yours? Would you feel as much compassion? What if the person were a complete stranger who, to your knowledge, had never done anything for or against you? Would your compassion be any greater or weaker? Perhaps it would be stronger than what you felt for your adversary. If it were a loved one drowning, could you even consider walking away and turning your back on the person? You would be besieged by the thought, 'How can I help this person out of this frightening situation?'

If we imagine this scenario vividly, it becomes quite clear that the compassion we feel for the person relies heavily on the type of relationship we have with them. Generally, the more drawn we are to someone, the more likely we are to have compassion for them.

Just imagining that someone is bound up and in danger of drowning arouses some compassion. Similarly, reflecting on the five features that characterise the plight of samsaric sentient beings helps us develop compassion for them. But the strength of our compassion may still differ, depending on whether a person is friend, foe or stranger. This partial type of compassion is not the great compassion required for the mind of enlightenment, for it is not based upon equanimity.

Cultivating equanimity through meditation

Developing equanimity helps us extend our loving concern to all in need of it. Ideally, the compassion we feel for all beings is of the same strength as the compassion we feel for someone dear to our heart. This is only possible if we feel drawn to them, finding in them something endearing and appealing.

Equanimity must come before great compassion because only then can we overcome our partiality and have care for all. Equanimity is a balanced attitude we cultivate towards friend, foe and stranger alike in order to stop the attachment, hostility and indifference we typically feel. It is an essential prerequisite to great compassion, which is in turn a primary cause for a mind of enlightenment.

There are different systems of cultivating equanimity.

Bodhicitta: the mind of enlightenment

We can focus on someone we are close to first, and then move on to a stranger and then an enemy; or we can meditate upon friend, enemy and stranger all at once. Either way is acceptable. Select a single person who is representative of each category.

When we turn our attention to the person we feel closest to, both affection and attachment arise. In cultivating equanimity for those we are close to we must first distinguish between, and then separate, attachment from affection. What is attachment? It is a state of mind that exaggerates the appeal of an object. It attributes positive qualities above and beyond what are actually there. Attachment makes us focus solely on the good points and blinds us to faults, so that later, when our attachment diminishes, the person or thing's faults become apparent and we struggle or become angry. Pure affection is genuine loving concern about another's well-being; it does not diminish when the person acts badly or contrary to our wishes.

Why are we attached to people and things? Underlying our attachment is the sense that this person helps me and brings me happiness. Though there are many other factors, these are the main ones. We have the sense that this person, from his or her own side, will make me happy.

We should consider this more closely. Does *the person* actually bring us happiness or does *the type of relationship* we have with the person determine that? Does this person always make me happy, or does it depend on the way we relate and interact? Upon investigation we find that the happiness does not simply come from the other person. These people do not *always* bring us happiness, do they? If the relationship takes a turn for the worse, the person will no longer make us happy. Where is the happiness when the relationship sours? If the happiness came from the person — and not the relationship — the person would brings us happiness despite worsening relations; but that is not the case.

Our attachment to this person attributes to them qualities above and beyond those they actually have, for instance, the ability to make us happy. It prevents us from seeing that the happiness we feel with regard to the person depends more on the relationship between the two of us. If we recognise this, we will not expect the person to make us happy. Our priority will become cultivating wholly positive relationships; that is, relationships based on loving concern and compassion, not attachment or other negative mental states. We will take a sincere interest in the other person's welfare and not use others for our own ends.

Our attachment prevents us from seeing a person as they are. Seeing only the person's positive attributes, we ignore or forget what this person may have done earlier in life, to say nothing of past lives. We are taken aback and hurt when this person acts badly. We suffer when this person is harmed or in danger. The person does not always brings us happiness, as our attachment would have it; far from it, in fact. Recognising this, we can overcome our attachment to the person without losing our affection or concern. This then gives us a solid basis for developing great compassion.

Next we turn our attention to someone we are indifferent towards. We feel indifferent because we do not consider them important. Perhaps we feel they are insignificant. It may be that we think we have no particular relationship with them, or else we don't recognise the relationship that we do have. There are many, many small creatures that fall into this category — for example, mosquitoes, ants, cockroaches and mice. We don't give much thought to their plight or how we treat them. It is our relationship with them or lack of it that shapes the way we feel about them.

We have a positive relationship with the people we are attached to. Believing that they bring us happiness, we consider them important and not insignificant. Yet any of these small creatures could also become quite significant to us. People keep mice as pets; if the mouse gets sick the owner takes it to the veterinary surgeon for treatment. A person may go to great lengths to look after a small mouse.

Clearly, changing the way we relate to others changes the way we regard them, and vice versa. What was once insignificant suddenly becomes important and dear. Though I have never met anybody who holds cockroaches to be dear, I have certainly seen people who feel that way towards mice.

There is no need to talk at length about the people we dislike, our enemies or adversaries. It is obvious that we get angry with them, believing they bring us harm and suffering. But if the relationship changes they cease to be our enemy and might even become our friend!

Sentient beings are, by nature, the same, but the type of relationship we have with them determines how we feel about them: attached, angry or indifferent. Knowing this, we need to change the way we relate to them. We can do this by thinking more deeply about their situation and ours.

We can only accomplish consummate personal well-being in dependence upon others. Our own well-being depends on our efforts to improve the well-being of others. When we can effortlessly and spontaneously accomplish the well-being of others, our own well-being will be complete. To do that, we must cultivate great loving-kindness and great compassion and that depends upon others. Our own well-being, to say nothing of our wisdom, compassion and ability, cannot be perfected as long as we are trapped by attachment, anger and indifference.

Maybe you are suspicious. Maybe you are thinking, 'I can try very hard from my own side to develop equanimity and

Bodhicitta: the mind of enlightenment

concern for all other beings, but if they don't reciprocate, the relationship can't improve!' Many people might change their attitudes towards us when they notice that we have taken a greater interest in their well-being. But even if they don't, changing the way we relate to them can still be very worthwhile. From our side, we will be happier now and in the future. The value of equanimity is not determined solely by the response we get from others.

We train the mind and cultivate equanimity to get rid of the partial or biased attitude we have towards others, to overcome the way we hold some close and others distant. We do this so that we feel, from our own side, loving-kindness and compassion for all sentient beings; so that we can treat them better. Even if another person is nasty and hurtful to us we do not need to lose our loving-kindness and compassion for them.

Our emphasis is on changing our own minds and behaviour; we cannot control others. If, despite the fact that we do all we can from our side, they continue to treat us badly, we should think about why they act like this. They act that way because they are suffering and because they are controlled by disturbing emotions. In fact they deserve our compassion not our anger!

To become a buddha we must develop consummate compassion, which in turn depends upon great compassion extended towards all sentient beings who are tormented by suffering. This type of unbiased compassion is based upon equanimity. Attachment, anger and indifference prejudice us towards or against others; they lead to a one-sided and limited compassion.

If we investigate why we are attached to friends, hostile to enemies and indifferent to strangers, we find these sentiments have no solid foundation. They are based upon mistaken thinking. They assume that others give us happiness and suffering, when in fact they depend on the way we relate to them! Furthermore, the categories of friend, foe and stranger are not rigid and unchanging. Even in this life a person can start out in one and end up in another.

The key to undermining our attachment, anger and indifference is to see how they are misguided and mistaken. There is no good reason we should be attached to some and angry or indifferent towards others. From their side, they all want to be happy and do not want to suffer. And from our side, our own happiness depends on them; can we really be happy if we bounce between anger, attachment and indifference? Can we develop loving-kindness, compassion, generosity or patience without them?

Once we develop equanimity, all sentient beings can appeal to us. Feeling drawn to all sentient beings allows us to develop great compassion, which is a primary cause for the mind of enlightenment. But before great compassion, we must have empathetic loving-kindness. Empathetic loving-kindness [*yid du 'ong gi byams pa*] is a state of mind that feels drawn to all sentient beings and wishes that those who are deprived of happiness have happiness.

Empathy [*yid du 'ong ba'i blo*] literally means 'to feel drawn to' or 'to find appealing'. Traditionally, there are two techniques used to develop it. The first involves recognising how all sentient beings have been our mother and the second involves 'equalising and exchanging self for others'.

The sevenfold instruction on cause and effect
All sentient beings have been our mother

The first technique aims to develop empathetic loving-kindness by establishing that all beings have been our mothers. Generally, no one is kinder to us than our mother and so naturally we feel a sense of closeness to her and wish her well. If we can see that all sentient beings have been our mother in one or another of our countless rebirths, we can engender the same sentiments for all.

Not everyone feels so close to their mother. Sometimes a person's relationship with their mother gets worse with time, so that as adults the affection has been lost and there is a great distance between the two. This is by no means the rule, but it does occur on occasion. Yet despite the bad feeling and intervening troubles, in most cases there were years when the mother raised her child with loving care.

One of the shortcomings of anger is that it makes us forget the kindness of others. When we are angry with someone it is difficult to remember that this person has been kind to us. Let's say you are close friends with someone for ten years and after ten years they do something to anger you. If the anger is strong enough it might block out all the years of kindness, so you can think only of how this person wronged you. You might break off the friendship and begin to think of your old friend as a bad person. If the anger is intense enough it can drive a person to murder.

It is important to recall the kindness of our mother despite the mistakes she might have made since she raised us. Someone who has had major problems in the relationship with their parents may find it difficult to think like this. Sometimes a mother will make grave mistakes; if a mother is an ordinary sentient being she is bound to. She is bound to have flaws because, after all, she is like us, controlled by disturbing emotions and past actions. It is much better to recognise this and develop compassion for the mother than to nurse one's anger.

As we have seen, we consider others to be friends, adversaries or strangers depending on the type of relationship we have with them. When we look more closely we see that these categories are not fixed: a friend is not always a friend, a stranger does not always stay a stranger. So people are not established as friends or adversaries from their own side. Our attitudes and relationships establish them as such.

If, because of a negative relationship, you find it difficult to think of your mother as the kindest of all sentient beings, you may use someone else as the basis for this meditation. Perhaps you feel that no one has been kinder to you than your brother, sister, friend or partner. In this case, you can use that person as an illustration of how others are extremely kind.

Think how all sentient beings have been this type of person to us before, and engender a sense of affection and gratitude towards them. Think about the light feeling of joy that arises when we hear their name, catch sight of them or simply think of them. At some point we felt this for all others, when they were our mother, brother, sister, friend or partner. Though we may not be so close to them in this life, we once were, and past kindnesses are past kindnesses, whether they are a year old or lifetimes old. Try to extend the sense of closeness, affection and gratitude to all sentient beings.

Eventually the same joy and sentiment we feel at the mention of our dearest loved one will arise at the mention of our greatest adversary. This is what we want to happen. We want to feel empathy for all; we want to feel drawn to all sentient beings without exception.

Recalling the kindness

After recognising that all sentient beings have been our mother, the second step is to recall their kindness. This step is very much linked to the second technique: equalising and exchanging self for others, which is discussed on page 192. Both of these require us to appreciate the importance and great kindness of others.

As we have just seen, all sentient beings have been our mother and at that time were very kind. They carried us in their womb, putting our needs before theirs, enduring much discomfort to carry us to full term. After we were born, they lovingly raised us and made sure we got what we needed until we could look after ourselves. But even when they are not acting as our mother, sentient beings are extremely kind. The material resources that we enjoy are produced by others. They grow the food we eat, bottle the drinks we consume, make the clothes we wear, and build the houses we live in. Material goods, which are so vital to us and our happiness, come to us from the kindness of others.

Yet others are kind to us in a dharmic sense as well. Think about how consummate compassion is developed. We would like to have consummate compassion, but its development depends on all samsaric sentient beings. We must recognise that each and every being plays a part in helping us develop compassion to its utmost extent. If we were to omit even a single sentient being, consummate compassion would be impossible. Consummate compassion is an all-encompassing compassion, so each sentient being is integral to its development. So from a Dharma perspective, each living being is extremely important and kind.

We must also acquaint ourselves with the idea that samsaric sentient beings are controlled by disturbing emotions. They might act for or against us, but they are still under the sway of disturbing emotions. When they act negatively towards us, they do so because they are controlled by anger or envy or another disturbing emotion. Knowing that others are not free and autonomous, but rather controlled by disturbing emotions, helps us to develop compassion for them.

When another acts to harm us, we have a chance to practise patience. At the moment we don't like it when others act negatively towards us. Things would be different if we realised that they are giving us an excellent opportunity to practise patience. This is an opportunity our spiritual teachers cannot give us; without it we would never perfect patience. We cannot properly practise patience with someone who always treats us well. It's only those who make problems and try to harm us that give us the opportunity. Therefore, our adversaries and aggressors are particularly kind to us. Without them we would never develop consummate patience. The same is true of compassion, loving-kindness and cherishing others.

Buddhahood is a consummate state, a state in which these positive qualities have been developed to their utmost extent. Excluding a single sentient being from our patience or compassion makes such an accomplishment impossible. Only in buddahood is our personal well-being complete. Other sentient beings are extremely kind in that they support our attainment of buddhahood and make it possible to perfect our well-being. Recognising how kind and important they are helps us to feel drawn to them.

Wishing to repay the kindness

Recognising all sentient beings as one's mother, recalling their kindness and wishing to repay it helps us feel drawn to all sentient beings. From a worldly perspective, someone who helps us and makes us happy is considered kind. This is also true in a dharmic way, but there is more to it.

From a Dharma perspective, someone who supports the development of our compassion or patience is also kind. In giving us the opportunity to practise, they are giving us the chance to achieve lasting happiness. Sentient beings are a support for our practice since much of it focuses upon them.

We want to develop consummate compassion and they facilitate that; they are in fact indispensable for that. If we can appreciate this, we will find them appealing. We will be drawn to people who give us the opportunity to practise. As the glorious Chandrakirti said, when bodhisattvas are intent on developing their generosity, they feel tremendous joy simply from hearing a person call out, 'Please give!' It stands to reason that such a person intent on developing consummate compassion or the perfection of patience would be drawn to those who give them the opportunity to practise.

When we are aware of the kindness of others, the thought 'How can I repay them?' naturally arises. This is the worldly way too: a decent person will want to repay the kindness extended to them. But how do we do so? Sentient beings desire any number of things: some want food, others want money, some want companionship. Even if we knew their individual desires it would be difficult to provide for them. So in Dharma terms, the best way to repay kindness is to give what everyone wants: happiness and freedom from suffering. The wish to repay the kindness of others leads to the wish for their happiness and freedom from suffering, which means we are ready to develop loving-kindness and compassion.

In this way equanimity helps us overcome partiality and bias, so our concern extends to all beings. The recognition that all sentient beings have been our mother makes us aware of their kindness, which in turn makes us want to repay them. Thinking in this way we begin to feel drawn to all sentient beings and lay the foundation for empathetic loving-kindness and great compassion.

Empathetic loving-kindness, great compassion and the highest intention

It is possible that we might work hard at developing an empathetic loving-kindness that is drawn to all sentient beings, but then stop there. But if we stop and do not sustain it our mind will not become so familiar with it. Once we succeed in generating it, we should work to maintain it so that it becomes second nature and uncontrived.

Analytical meditation is used to both generate and accustom ourselves to loving-kindness. Analytical meditations use reason and logic to develop conviction and faith. When doing analytical meditation on loving-kindness for instance, a person thinks about the nature of loving-kindness, what its focus and aspect are, what advantages there are in cultivating it, and so on. This is different in some ways from placement meditation. Placement meditation tends to focus on a single object continuously, while analytical meditation often goes through a sequence of objects related to a single topic. Both are meant to increase our familiarity with the object of meditation, but they do so in different ways. Analytical meditation generally comes first because we must know an object well before we can place our minds single-pointedly on it.

The difference between generating and accustoming is simply that in the first case we are trying to arouse loving-kindness from an unmanifest state and in the second we are trying to maintain a manifest state for as long as possible so that our familiarity with it increases. The mind needs time and repetition to get used to things. Eventually it will become second nature.

Loving-kindness means we wish that all sentient beings be happy. Yet we know that as long as we suffer we will not be totally happy, so naturally we also wish that they be free of suffering. Compassion arises automatically from loving-kindness when we recognise that happiness mixed with suffering is an incomplete happiness. Compassion, the wish that all sentient beings be free of suffering, is a natural extension of our loving-kindness.

Having developed empathetic loving-kindness and great compassion, we must continue to cultivate them so our familiarity with them deepens. At a certain point the wish for the happiness of others, and that they be free of suffering, becomes so strong that it overwhelms us. Overwhelmed and unable to stand by without doing anything we think, 'I myself must free them from suffering and establish them in happiness. It is my personal responsibility.' This is the highest intention. When we reach this point we have made the transition from simply wanting something for others to taking responsibility to see that they get it.

In assuming this responsibility we must ask ourselves a question: 'Do I have the ability to realise my wishes?' Inevitably, we conclude that we do not, at present, have the ability to free all sentient beings from suffering and establish them in unchanging happiness. Aware of our limitations we begin to see the need for buddhahood, a state of consummate wisdom, compassion and ability. But surely such a state is not easily accomplished. We must ask, 'Is it at all possible to attain such a state?'

It is easier to see the need for buddhahood than it is to prove that such a state is possible. To prove that, we must understand what prevents us from developing the qualities of wisdom, compassion and ability to their utmost extent, namely, grasping at true existence and self-cherishing. If we can prove that these obstacles can be removed, we can prove the possibility of attaining buddhahood. To do that we must understand how grasping at true existence is a wrong awareness and how cherishing others undermines self-cherishing.

A strong conviction in and dedication to attaining buddhahood comes from resolving that it is not only possible, but in fact necessary, to attain buddhahood. If we want to be free from suffering and establish others in perfect happiness, we must attain it. If we eliminate ignorance and self-cherishing, we can attain it. Only then will we be able to act fully upon the highest intentions of loving-kindness and compassion.

The highest intention leads directly to the mind of enlightenment, a mind that wants to attain consummate wisdom, compassion and the ability to alleviate the suffering of all sentient beings.

It is vital that we prepare ourselves to face difficult situations before we actually encounter them. Cultivating loving-kindness, compassion and patience when we are relaxed helps us to apply them when challenged. Understanding the need for them and how they are reasonable responses will give us strength even if we have not spent a great deal of time meditating on them. It helps to understand that retribution and retaliation perpetuate an endless cycle of harm and suffering. Knowing that sentient beings are controlled by disturbing emotions — and thus are not in complete control — helps us resist their influence and encourages compassion for others. Cultivating these in meditation helps us develop further stability and strength. First we must understand, then we must meditate.

There is a difference between being displeased and being angry. Being displeased or upset is not the same as being angry; but becoming displeased often leads to becoming angry. Anger involves ill will. If we nurse our displeasure there is the danger we will want revenge. The moment ill will or malice arises, our displeasure has become anger. To avoid this, we can remember that the harm others cause us stems from their own suffering and the fact that they are controlled by disturbing emotions. They need our compassion, not our anger. Developing goodwill rather than ill will purifies the negative seeds placed in the mind by past moments of ill will. This is the best way to purify such seeds and the best way to ensure happiness.

Equalising and exchanging self for others

We have only referred briefly to the second technique, equalising and exchanging self for others. In this practice, we try to recognise the disadvantages of self-cherishing and the advantages of cherishing others. Knowing the shortcomings of the one and the value of the other helps us to exchange our self-cherishing for a mind that cherishes others. This is what it means to 'exchange self for others.' It is called 'equalising self and other' because we must first cultivate equanimity before we can exchange the two attitudes. While in some ways this second technique is the more difficult, it does not require us to think about past and future rebirths.

In applying this technique we are seeking to exchange our self-cherishing for a mind that cherishes others. But why would we want to do that? Self-cherishing is the main obstacle to developing a mind of enlightenment. If there is one thing incompatible with a mind of enlightenment it is self-cherishing. Self-cherishing is said to be the gateway to all troubles, while cherishing others is the foundation of all Mahayana qualities.

Does this confuse you? Surely we must care for and look after ourselves, so why must we get rid of self-cherishing?

There are actually two types of self-cherishing. The first cherishes oneself to the exclusion of others. The second type does not neglect others and is not supported by the misapprehension of self. Someone with this second type of self-cherishing is quite careful not to harm others. Some people seek to benefit themselves regardless of the effect that has on others. Others are more conscientious, but still concerned mainly with their own welfare. Some put others before self, like a bodhisattva or buddha.

The first type of self-cherishing is the gateway to all troubles. It stands in direct opposition to a mind of enlightenment. Selfishly seeking benefit for oneself, regardless of how that harms others, creates suffering for both oneself and others. It is obvious how our indifference hurts others: if we don't care about the plight of others we are unlikely to refrain from actions that harm them. But how does this create suffering for ourselves?

The problems and sufferings we encounter are the results of non-virtuous actions. Non-virtuous actions include killing, stealing, sexual misconduct, and speaking harshly or falsely to others. Such harmful and non-virtuous actions are based on cherishing self above others. Killing provides a useful example. A person may kill out of anger or attachment, but to do so they must put their interests over the victim's. They must neglect the victim's life and well-being to kill. If we are indifferent to another person or animal, we are more likely to neglect its well-being, particularly when we think we stand to gain.

Physical and mental suffering come from negative actions. Negative actions depend on some degree of indifference to others. Cherishing one's own well-being above that of others leads to neglect and indifference. Thus, self-cherishing is the gateway to all troubles.

To recap, there are two types of self-cherishing: one is rude and inconsiderate, the other is not. Cherishing oneself to the exclusion of others and being indifferent to their welfare is something we must overcome. But do not think this means we should cease caring about our own health and well-being! If we get sick, we should see a doctor. When it is cold we should put on warm clothes. We should exercise and eat well and work so that we have enough money to live comfortably. The point of abandoning self-cherishing is to overcome our selfish indifference to others so that we may cherish them as dearly as we do ourselves. Basically the negative form of self-cherishing is selfish indifference to others.

From a Buddhist perspective, all sentient beings, ourselves included, are basically equal. We want to be happy and do not want to suffer; the same can be said for others. And though they seek happiness they do not know how to create its causes and fail to achieve their desires; though they do not want to suffer, they do not know how to abandon its causes, and unwittingly create more suffering. However, as an individual, you are just one sentient being whereas other sentient beings are limitless, like space. Collectively, their welfare outweighs your own and so you should not pursue your own well-being at their expense. Thinking like this, you can even hold them more dear than yourself. Knowing this, we should develop compassion for all sentient beings, for although we are all fundamentally equal, the countless multitudes deserve more consideration and help than any single person.

From this perspective, to cherish oneself above others is to neglect others and in turn create more suffering. We may not understand the subtle causes for our physical and mental suffering but we have direct experience of the way indifference to others only makes things worse. Think of the last quarrel you were in. How did it start? Was it because one person was selfishly indifferent to another? What about family squabbles? Don't most of them come down to one person putting their wants in front of another's? Isn't this the case with almost all problems and difficulties in our lives?

If we look honestly and objectively at our lives, none of us could deny that selfish indifference creates problems big and small. Whether we practice Buddhism or not, we must all pay attention to this. Anyone who acts on this will be happier as a result.

What does it mean to 'cherish others'? The strongest form of cherishing others regards countless other beings as more important than oneself. This attitude is the foundation of all Mahayana qualities, like loving-kindness and compassion. For how could we intentionally harm someone if our equanimity were stable and we strongly cherished others? With this attitude we wouldn't act maliciously or do something negative without reason. A mind that cherishes others is a support for ethics, generosity and patience, to say nothing of loving-kindness, compassion, the highest intention and the mind of enlightenment.

Buddhist ethics and conduct are based on the philosophy of not harming others. The most basic form of Buddhist ethics is called abandoning the ten non-virtues. The ten non-virtues are actions that harm not just oneself but others as well. They are killing, stealing and sexual misconduct; speaking harshly, falsely, divisively and idly; and having ill will, covetousness and wrong views. Thus from a Buddhist perspective, observing ethics involves abandoning or refraining from these ten acts.

Cherishing others not only helps us observe ethics and not harm others but also helps us increase goodwill and kindness, the basis of the Mahayana. Thus it is the foundation of all Mahayana qualities.

The distinction between a negative self-cherishing and

Bodhicitta: the mind of enlightenment

a non-harming, decent one relates to a basic difference between the Mahayana and Hinayana. Giving up ill will and not harming others is the foundation of Buddhism in general and the Hinayana in particular. Working for the sake of others is the foundation of the Mahayana. While both traditions abandon ill will and cultivate compassion, the emphasis in their practice differs.

Self-cherishing is not a wrong awareness in the same way as the misapprehension of self. In fact a person can achieve liberation without abandoning self-cherishing. But when self-cherishing teams up with the misapprehension of self — and ill will — a rude and inconsiderate state of mind is the result. Since the two together cause havoc, Buddhist practitioners try to separate them. Whether the person chooses to abandon self-cherishing or the misapprehension of self first depends upon their orientation and inclination.

What happens when a misapprehension of self and ill will support self-cherishing? Say a mosquito lands on our arm. Thinking that it will inject us with a poison that makes our arm itch or that it carries some disease, we decide to kill it, without considering the mosquito's state. We ignore the fact that this mosquito needs blood for one reason or another or that its existence must be a miserable one. We are indifferent to its plight and so we kill it. Though we need to care for ourselves, we do not need this rude and inconsiderate type of self-cherishing. We ordinary beings do need to cherish ourselves to a certain degree, but in a decent and considerate way. So what we can do is try to avoid being bitten in the first place, by applying mosquito repellent, wearing long sleeves, or putting up screens, for example.

Self-cherishing leads to anger, hostility, pride, envy and attachment. Though self-cherishing itself is not a wrong awareness, it leads to wrong awarenesses. What does this mean? Simply put, when we are self-cherishing we cannot bear any harm being done to ourself; we think constantly of how to avoid suffering. When we combine self-cherishing with indifference to others, we might use others to achieve our own happiness; when we combine self-cherishing with ill will, we may be willing to hurt others to get what we want.

Rude as it may be, self-cherishing technically is not a wrong awareness. A wrong awareness is an awareness whose object does not exist. It erroneously apprehends an object so in effect its object does not exist, or at least does not exist in the way the wrong awareness holds it to. Since it is in error, it is called 'wrong'. Consider the case of a person who looks at a snow-capped mountain while wearing blue-tinted sunglasses. Although the snow is white, it appears to be blue. If the person then assumes that snow is blue, he or she would have a 'wrong' awareness. The object of self-cherishing is one's own happiness. Self-cherishing might not care about the plight of others, but wanting happiness and not wanting to suffer are not wrong, they are not errors.

However, disturbing emotions that depend on self-cherishing are wrong awarenesses. Attachment exaggerates the appeal of its object and anger exaggerates the unattractiveness of its object. They are in error, and so are wrong. But the fact that self-cherishing is not a wrong awareness does not mean that it is harmless. As we have seen, it is the gateway to all troubles.

Meditating on the two techniques

As previously mentioned, the first technique for developing a mind of enlightenment is called the sevenfold instruction on cause and effect. We have been discussing the first six instructions, which are causes leading to the seventh, an effect — a mind of enlightenment. What is the best way to practise these? Is it better to meditate on all seven each day? Or should we focus on clarifying one before moving on to the next?

If you work and cannot spend your days in meditation, it might be good to meditate on all seven each day. Every week or every month you may shift your focus from one to the next, so the first week most of your time is spent meditating on equanimity, the second week on recognising that all sentient beings have been your mother, etc. In the time remaining, go through the other stages in order, spending a short time, not just a fleeting moment, on each. But the majority of your time ought to be spent on that week or that month's focus.

We never know when we will die and we don't want our practice of these seven to be incomplete. We want to have some familiarity with each stage before we die and that is why this is such a good approach. Focus on one and meditate briefly on the others. After a week or month devoted to equanimity, spend most of your time on recognising all sentient beings as your mother. Continue like this.

If you have a large amount of time to meditate each day, it may be best to focus entirely on one before moving on. Start with equanimity and continue until you have a very clear sense that, from your side and from theirs, all sentient beings are basically the same and there are no good reasons why we should be attached to some, angry with others and indifferent towards the rest. Then move on to the second stage and so on.

Decide which approach is best for you and stick to it. If you apply yourself each day you will certainly notice changes in your thoughts and actions. And, most importantly, your efforts will have well prepared you to cultivate a positive, virtuous mind at the time of death.

7

The correct view

As ordinary beings, we are controlled by our disturbing emotions. They motivate us to act in negative ways that create suffering for ourselves. If we could free ourselves from these disturbing emotions we would be free of the suffering and problems that are traced back to them. To free ourselves from disturbing emotions, we must free ourselves from the ignorance that underpins them. Ignorance, in particular ignorance of the nature of the self, lies at the root of disturbing emotions; by uprooting it, we uproot disturbing emotions. So the issue is, how do we overcome ignorance?

Knowledge and wisdom counter ignorance. If misunderstanding the self lies at the root of our problems, the solution must lie in correctly understanding the self. To do that, we must recognise the incorrect way we perceive and think about all things, including the self. After all, to rectify an error we must first identify the error that has been made! Correct view correctly sees the nature of the self as it is, empty of an independent 'self'. It is not only free from error; it destroys the causes of error. By developing wisdom of the correct view, and realising emptiness, we uproot the fundamental cause of suffering and wash away that which comes from it. In this chapter we look at verses 9 to 14 of *The Three Principal Aspects of the Path*.

Verses 9 to 14 of
The Three Principal Aspects of the Path

Why we need correct view

9   *If you don't have wisdom realising the way things are,*
      Even though you familiarise yourself with renunciation and bodhicitta
      You won't be able to cut the root of samsara.
      So use every means to realise interdependence.

Meaning of correct view

10   *When you see that for all phenomena in samsara and nirvana*
      Cause and effect is unfailing
      And the object of fixation perishes,
      That is when you've entered the path that pleases the buddhas.

Incomplete correct view

11   *Appearances — dependent arisings — are unfailing*
      And emptiness is free of assertions.
      As long as these two seem to you disparate
      You have not yet realised the intent of Shakyamuni.

Complete correct view

12   *At some point in time, suddenly, they cease to alternate*
      And just by seeing that interdependence is unfailing
      A certainty that destroys all misapprehensions comes about.
      At that time your analysis of the view is complete.

13 Furthermore, appearances clear away the extreme of
         existence and
    Emptiness clears away the extreme of non-existence.
    When you understand how emptiness shows itself as cause
         and result
    You can never be held captive by extreme views.

14 When you realise as I have the crux
    Of the three principal aspects of the path explained here,
    Then, my child, stay in isolation, persevere with joy and
    Quickly accomplish the perfect goal that lies ahead.

The moon goes through phases over the course of a lunar month. The lunar month begins with the new moon when none of the moon can be seen. After a few days a small portion becomes visible and with each passing day this portion grows bigger and bigger. Eventually the face of the moon is seen in full. The process of developing the correct view and becoming a buddha is a lot like this.

Why cultivate correct view?

Why should we cultivate the correct view — the wisdom realising the ultimate nature of things? The reason is explained in the ninth verse:

> *If you don't have wisdom realising the way things are,*
> *Even though you familiarise yourself with renunciation and bodhicitta*
> *You won't be able to cut the root of samsara.*
> *So use every means to realise interdependence.*

The path to enlightenment integrates both method and wisdom. Both renunciation and the mind of enlightenment are aspects of 'method' as opposed to 'wisdom'. Renunciation is a method for attaining liberation, the mind of enlightenment a method for attaining enlightenment. But wisdom must assist them if either is to be attained. Method alone is not enough — we need its counterpart, wisdom.

Renunciation, loving-kindness, compassion and patience can prevent disturbing emotions from becoming manifest, but they cannot eliminate such emotions from the mind altogether. Only a wisdom that realises emptiness can cut the root of cyclic existence and destroy suffering and its seeds. By exposing the error in grasping at an inherently existent self, wisdom undermines ignorance and the disturbing emotions that rely on it.

How can we realise emptiness? The easiest way to realise emptiness is by realising the truth of interdependence or dependent arising. We will easily comprehend emptiness once we have realised interdependence. This is why Lama Tsongkhapa advises us to 'use every means to realise interdependence' first.

We touched on interdependence in Chapter 6, when talking about equanimity. Though it seems to us that others bring us happiness, upon further investigation we find that happiness arises in dependence upon the relationship we have with them. Quite often, this does not dawn on us. Rather, we attribute our happiness to them, thinking, 'This person *makes* me so happy.' So when the object of our affection does something to make us suffer, we are amazed; we cannot understand what has happened. The world crumbles around us and, bewildered, we are driven to distraction. Our belief that happiness comes from others makes us overlook the dependent nature of happiness, hence the surprise.

Interdependence has different levels. The coarsest level is to arise in dependence upon causes and conditions; more subtle than that is to be established in dependence upon parts; and finally the most subtle is to be established in dependence upon a basis for designation.

The first is the easiest to realise since we see it happening all around us, in the environment and surrounds. For instance, it is easy to see that a tree arises in dependence upon causes and conditions. To grow, it needs a seed, soil, water, sunlight and nutrients. All effects depend on causes and conditions, the most important of which is the unique substantial cause, without which the effect could not arise. Even the most insignificant pleasures and pains could not possibly arise without a substantial cause. That such things arise in dependence upon causes and conditions proves that they do not inherently exist, in and of themselves.

Functioning things, whether internal or external, cannot

arise in total isolation from other factors. Functioning things necessarily depend on other factors for their production. Functioning things, like non-functioning phenomena, possess parts; they could not exist without these parts.

There is a debate in Buddhist philosophy about whether 'partless particles' exist. This theory of a basic building-block of the universe is familiar to science. For years, scientists have been trying to divide increasingly small particles to determine whether there is an indivisible component of matter. If such a thing were found it might be considered in science a 'partless particle', for it could not be reduced into smaller parts. In Buddhism, a partless particle is one that is not composed of parts. There is a difference.

Certain Buddhist schools have maintained that any coarse material object can be divided into parts until you arrive at the incredibly small 'partless particle'. Higher Buddhist schools argue that there is no such thing as a partless particle because an atom, quark or whatever, regardless of its size, can still be mentally dissected into parts. For instance, if a supposedly partless particle were placed on a surface, wouldn't one part touch the surface and another part not? Wouldn't there also be northerly, easterly, southerly and westerly quarters? Could this particle exist without these parts? No. Since anything that possesses parts depends on those parts — and no thing is wholly partless — things do not inherently exist. If a thing

The correct view

is established in dependence upon its parts it does not exist inherently, but why?

A car is established in dependence upon a collection of parts. None of the parts alone is the car. Is the window the car? Is the door the car? Are the seats the car? No. The collection of parts is not the car either. Disassemble a car and pile its parts in a heap. Is this collection of parts a car? No. If a car existed inherently it ought to exist independent from these parts, but where is the car without its parts?

The subtlest level of interdependence is that phenomena are established in dependence upon a basis of designation. Take the example of a horse-drawn cart, as Nagarjuna did. There is no horse-drawn cart without the wheels and body and other parts that are the bases for designating it. Yet neither the wheel nor the body are the horse-drawn cart, so what is this horse-drawn cart? It is something imputed in dependence upon the collection of parts that are a basis for its designation.

Phenomena are established through being labelled or designated onto a basis of designation. This is true for anything that exists, be it permanent and unchanging or impermanent and in flux. Since everything is established in dependence upon a basis of designation, nothing exists inherently. Phenomena exist imputedly but not inherently. That is, they are established through the imputation or designation of names and concepts and not without that.

Emptiness is the final status of all phenomena. All phenomena are empty of inherent existence and this is their most subtle mode of being. Emptiness, or selflessness, is divided into two categories, depending on what type of phenomenon forms the basis for emptiness: selflessness of persons and selflessness of phenomena.

In Buddhist terms, anything that exists is a called a 'phenomenon'. A phenomenon might be a person or something other than a person. A person's lack of inherent existence is called 'selflessness of persons'. The lack of inherent existence of a phenomenon other than person is called 'selflessness of phenomena'. So although a 'person' is a phenomenon, the 'selflessness of person' is not a 'selflessness of phenomena'. The two are not the same. These subtle types of selflessness are not different types of emptiness, per se. They differ solely in terms of the subject that forms the basis for emptiness — person or otherwise. Still, it is easier to realise selflessness of persons because it is easier to see how the 'self of persons' is an imputed existent.

'Person' is a term that refers not just to humans but to all beings. For simplicity's sake, we can say that all persons have a body and a mind. The body and mind are the bases for the designating, imputing or labelling a 'person'. A person depends on the body and mind collection; it does not exist apart from, or independent of, body and mind. In fact, a 'person' is merely imputed or labelled onto body and mind and does not exist from their side.

If a person existed from the side of its body and mind, either body or mind would have to be the person. But a body is not the person, nor is a mind the person. Otherwise why would we talk about 'my body, my mind and me'? Such worldly conventions tell us that 'I' am not reducible to body or mind. Yet what am 'I' without body and mind? What is the 'I', this self that exists in dependence on body and mind but is not body or mind? The 'I' is an imputed existent, established through being labelled onto body and mind. A person does not exist from the side of body and mind because it is imputed onto them, like a car or a horse-drawn cart. A horse-drawn cart does not inherently exist and neither does a person.

It seems to us as if 'I' exist as an entity independent of 'my' body and mind. But where is the 'I' apart from body and mind? There is none, for 'I' exist in dependence upon 'my' body and mind. Yet neither my body nor my mind *is* me. Body and mind are the bases for designating me. I am merely labelled onto body and mind.

Emptiness is not just a distant metaphysical concept but the very nature of the things that surround us in the world. The conventions of the world uphold emptiness. Take, for example, a library. Does a building inherently exist as a library? Or is a library established through giving a label to a building and its contents? Before there is a library, walls must be built, pillars erected, windows installed, books brought in and shelved. These are the bases for designating the building a 'library'.

Does the building exist as a library from its own side? Are the walls the library? Are the pillars the library? Are the books the library? No, no, no. If the building inherently existed as a library, it could never be anything else. But maybe the community will outgrow the library, build a new one, and use the old one as a community centre. At that point it is no longer a library but a community centre.

A library is merely labelled onto the bases for its designation. But a library is not just a mere label, because you can sit in it and borrow books from it. It is not that a 'library' does not exist at all; rather, it does not exist as it seems to. It seems to be an independent entity but it is in fact a dependent and imputed entity. If left unexamined, you can quite happily make use of the library and its services. But if you are not satisfied with this 'merely labelled library' and inquire further, you will find no library! Where exactly, in all those parts, is the library?

That you can sit in a library shows that it exists. That you cannot find it in its parts shows that it does not exist from its own side. A similar inquiry into the nature of self reveals that 'I' am merely labelled onto the body and mind collection and do not exist from the side of body and mind. Let us think a bit more about the 'library.' Is a library an entity distinct from the basis for designating it? Is it identical to that basis? It cannot be a distinct entity because if you destroy the windows, walls, and contents there is no longer any library to speak of. There is no library apart from those things. Does that mean a library is identical to those things? No, because none of those things individually is the library. We may be across the road and point at a building, saying, 'That is the library,' but we cannot pinpoint any single thing in there that is the library.

The same can be said of the person. We instinctually have a sense of self or individual identity. Yet the 'I' that we assume to exist is different from the 'I' that actually exists. We operate as if the self were an inherently existent entity, existing apart from body and mind. But the self does not inherently exist as body or mind; nor does it exist as an entity distinct from the two.

The 'I' is imputed onto body and mind, which means that it exists in dependence upon them and is a single entity with them. Like the library that is not identical to its parts yet does not exist apart from them, the 'I' is not identical to body or mind, nor is it a wholly different entity. It is an imputed phenomenon that exists in dependence upon body and mind.

Why then does the self appear to be something independent of body and mind? When we think of 'my body and my mind', why does the 'I' seem to be a third entity, distinct from the other two? It is a false appearance created by our instinctual misapprehension of self. Whether we intellectually believe that the self exists inherently or not, on a subtle and innate level, we apprehend it to be so. This instinctual misapprehension of self creates the appearance of an inherently existent self so that 'I' do not appear to be dependently designated. Rather the 'I' seems to exist truly, an entity distinct from body and mind.

The instinctual misapprehension of self is produced together with mind. Accompanying mind without beginning, it taints and obscures the mind so that everything that appears to our perception and our conceptual mind appears to exist from its own side. What we perceive through our senses and what we conceive in our thoughts seems to inherently exist; not just our own self, but the selves of others, our bodies and all things.

Why is this important? This subtle ignorance is the root of our suffering and cyclic existence. To stop suffering and be free of cyclic existence we must realise how this misapprehension is wrong. We must realise that we grasp at the self, holding it to exist from its own side when in fact it is imputed onto body and mind. To overcome the misapprehension, we must know where it errs, must realise that although we apprehend things to inherently exist, they are empty of inherent existence. Our instinctual misapprehension of self grasps at an object that doesn't exist, namely an inherently existent 'I'. Emptiness disproves or refutes that type of 'I'. We cannot realise emptiness until we have identified that object.

There are certain moments when that object becomes abundantly clear. For instance, in moments of great anger, we have a strong sense of a stand-alone 'I', independent of body and mind. If another person wrongfully accuses us of some vile act, we are likely to think, 'How dare they accuse *me! I* did not do that!' In the heat of the moment, does it ever occur to us that 'I' am merely labelled onto body and mind and that there is no concrete and independent self? No! If we look at our sense of self when we become angry, we will see the 'I' as the misapprehension of self holds it to be.

There is a discrepancy between the way the 'I' appears and the way it actually exists. To realise emptiness we must understand that the way in which relative phenomena like the self appear is incompatible with the way they are, like the reflection of a face in a mirror. A face appears to be in the mirror, though it is not. The self appears to exist inherently, though it does not. The great master Gungthang Jampelyang said that we must look into the immediate appearances at hand to discover how we misapprehend things, otherwise we will never find what we are looking for. In other words, the fundamental error of ignorance can be found in our immediate experiences. The object negated by emptiness does not lie elsewhere.

With a deep and detailed experiential understanding, masters of the past taught that things do not exist as they appear. Though we instinctually grasp at a self that seems to inherently exist apart from body and mind, there is no such self. We fail to apprehend that the self is actually merely labelled onto body and mind. The self is not identical to body and mind, nor is it a distinct entity. The middle ground between these two is quite subtle. The self is merely labelled but is not a mere label. It is not easy to develop the wisdom that realises selflessness. The perfection of wisdom is inexpressible, inconceivable and indescribable.

Misapprehending the self and the wisdom that realises selflessness

The wisdom that realises selflessness is the root of true freedom and liberation. The misapprehension of self is the root of cyclic existence. How is wisdom a remedy for misapprehension? The misapprehension of self grasps at an inherently existent person, while the wisdom that realises selflessness realises that there is no inherently existent person. In other

The correct view

words, the misapprehension grasps at an object that does not exist, which the wisdom recognises as wrong and thereby overcomes.

Both misapprehension and wisdom are focused on the self of person, but the ways they hold it to exist are diametrically opposed. The misapprehension wrongly grasps at the 'I', holding it to exist from its own side. The wisdom recognises that the self does not exist from the side of body and mind but rather is designated onto them. The first is erroneous and wrong. The second is valid and accurate. By acquainting ourselves with a valid apprehension of the self's lack of inherent existence we can eliminate the misapprehension that grasps at a non-existent person. Only by familiarising ourselves with what validly exists can we stop grasping at what does not; there is no other way.

Reciting mantras, making aspirational prayers, circumambulating holy objects and making offerings are meritorious and are all wonderful supports for wisdom. We might recite millions upon millions of *mani* mantras, pray day and night without sleeping, circumambulate a stupa millions of times, but still we would not be able to eliminate the misapprehension of self. Only familiarity with the wisdom that realises selflessness can do that.

As Shantideva says, we can collect merit by practising the first perfections and all the while strive for wisdom. The first five perfections of generosity, ethics, patience, joyous effort and concentration provide a support and stability for the sixth, the perfection of wisdom. I do not mean to disparage prayer; I only want to point out that we must develop wisdom even as we gather merit.

I would encourage you to reflect on these teachings in light of your own experience. Compare and contrast what you hear and read with what you've learned in your life. With time, you may get a taste of the Dharma and be able to integrate it into your life. This is very important.

The tenth verse reads:

When you see that for all phenomena in samsara and nirvana
Cause and effect is unfailing
And the object of fixation perishes,
That is when you've entered the path that pleases the buddhas.

The principle of cause and effect is not limited to samsara, to cyclic existence. Its reach extends into nirvana, the liberated state beyond all sorrow. Since no effect can arise without a cause of similar type, cause and effect are equally incontrovertible or unfailing in nirvana as they are in samsara. If we realise this level of interdependence we will realise that the object the misapprehension of self grasps at does not exist and that is why it is said to have been destroyed.

The correct view

Before we can destroy our instinctual misapprehension of self we must recognise the object it grasps at. This object, a truly or inherently existent 'I', is its reference point and it does not exist. Destroying the reference point is only the first step in destroying the misapprehension itself.

The conception of an inherently existent self is the mainstay of our instinctual misapprehension of self. The misapprehension holds the self to be independent of causes and conditions. This independent self is its reference point. The realisation that no functioning thing, including the self, is independent of causes and conditions destroys this false reference point, undermining the misapprehension. This is the path that pleases the buddhas.

Once we have understood that we grasp at an inherently existent self where no such self exists, we must cultivate that understanding in meditation. It is not enough simply to understand. We must stabilise and deepen our understanding. Continue to question your understanding in order to remove doubts; refine the clarity of your understanding and increase your familiarity with it.

Search body and mind. Can you find a discrete self anywhere? The self and all other phenomena are merely labelled onto a basis of designation. When you look for a 'thing' among those bases there is no 'thing' to find. Know all phenomena to be like this. Use analytical meditation to arrive at this understanding. When the meaning of selflessness becomes clear, allow your mind to dwell on it.

Initially your focus should be on analytical meditation interspersed with short periods of placement meditation. The quality of meditation is more important than its duration. When you place your mind on the meaning of selflessness, be sure that your mind is sharp and clear. As beginners we may try to meditate for too long, in which case our mind becomes dull and vague.

It is only through familiarity gained in meditation that we can dispel the obscurations. An intellectual understanding is necessary, but not enough on its own. First you must understand, then meditate on what you've understood. Continue to deepen your familiarity with that until emotional and cognitive obscurations have been removed.

The eleventh verse reads:

> *Appearances — dependent arisings — are unfailing*
> *And emptiness is free of assertions.*
> *As long as these two seem to you disparate*
> *You have not yet realised the intent of Shakyamuni.*

In his *In Praise of Dependent Arising*, Lama Tsongkhapa singles out dependent arising, praising it at length, saying that it is the very heart of Buddha Shakyamuni's teaching.[1] To say that

The correct view

dependent arising and emptiness are not disparate, or conflicting, is the same as saying that cause and effect are unfailing. The interdependence of cause and effect is readily seen. It surrounds us. We touch it with our hands and see it with our eyes. The view of emptiness does not harm it at all, in fact it supports it. There is no contradiction in saying that an effect does not inherently exist but does arise in dependence upon causes. If a thing arises in dependence upon other things it cannot exist inherently. And how could something that existed inherently arise in dependence upon causes and conditions? Dependent arising and emptiness are mutually supportive. As long as we see them as incompatible and fail to recognise their reciprocity, we have not found the correct view.

The correct view is not easy to find. It is difficult to see that the two are two sides of the same coin. Of all the schools of Buddhist philosophy, only the Middle Way Consequence school has fully uncovered it. The other tenet schools cannot explain how being interdependent and being empty of inherent existence necessarily complement each other.

Mind — the migrator from life to life — is intangible and immaterial. Even though we cannot see mind, no one denies that we are aware and sentient beings. Every being has the capacity for knowledge, the ability to know, feel, distinguish and act. This 'knower' of things is a mental entity, not a physical one, so Buddhists call it 'mind.' Mind is naturally and necessarily present in all sentient life.

When that mind animates a human body, we have a 'human'; when it animates a feline body, we have a 'cat'; when it animates a canine body, we have a 'dog'. Though the body changes, the nature of the mind — the basic capacity for awareness — is the same in all sentient life. The degree to which a being is capable of higher mental functioning depends in large part upon the physical support for mind. Some physical forms, like that of a human with a complex brain, support mental functioning of a much higher degree than, say, a fish. A fish's body can only support basic mental functions, so higher levels remain latent. Higher levels of mental functioning will not manifest in a fish even though its mind has the capacity for them because the fish's body and brain cannot support them. In short, all minds have the same basic potential, but the range of mental activity depends on the physical support, the body.

Wisdom and conviction come from learning, reflecting and meditating. At first we have doubts. As we read more and attend teachings, our doubts may be dispelled and our conviction may grow. We may go back and forth, thinking, 'Do things exist inherently or not?' We tend to think that they do not, but we are still not convinced; this is called doubt that tends towards the fact. We think more about these things until we conclude, 'Things cannot exist inherently. If they arise in dependence upon and in relation to other things, how could they?' At that point we have not yet realised emptiness but are convinced of it. Our inquiry continues until we remove all remaining doubts. The thoroughness of our analysis lends strength to our conviction and gives birth to wisdom. By meditating on what we've realised, we develop a wisdom borne of meditation. In this way we can realise the full potential of our human mind and become a buddha.

These days many people have low self-esteem. To help the person deal with this, Western psychologists often try to build up a person's sense of self. This is an acknowledged and successful technique but on the surface it seems to conflict with the Buddhist teachings on selflessness. This raises two questions: Are the two really in conflict? If not, is it useful for a person with a poor self-image to strengthen their sense of self before meditating on selflessness?

In response to the first question, we must distinguish between a self that exists and one that does not. For simplicity, let us call these the existent self and the non-existent self. The existent self is a self that is apprehended correctly, that is seen to be empty of inherent existence. This type of self exists conventionally and is called the 'mere I' since it is merely imputed onto body and mind.

The non-existent self is a self that is held to exist

inherently, from its own side. In observing the 'mere I' we instinctually take it to exist inherently, thereby grasping at a non-existent self. There is no inherently existent self, is there? There is no such thing as a self that exists from its own side, not conventionally, not nominally.

The teachings on selflessness negate only the non-existent self, not the conventionally existent 'mere I'. So if the existent and non-existent selves are properly distinguished, the two approaches are not necessarily in conflict. However, teaching emptiness to a person who is not prepared for it violates the vows of a bodhisattva. We must be careful not to teach emptiness to someone who has not trained and prepared their mind for it. Knowing this, I was hesitant to teach emptiness in Australia, even though many people requested me to. I sought advice from His Holiness the Dalai Lama, who encouraged me to teach and emphasised how important it is for people to understand emptiness properly.

In general, however, teachings on emptiness should not be given too freely. If a person is not receptive to the idea of an existent self alongside a non-existent self, it is difficult to discuss this topic with them. The person must be broad-minded enough to explore the idea fully and objectively. Just as importantly, they ought to be inclined to reflect on such ideas and be in a fit state to do so. The teachings on selflessness can be beneficial but only if the circumstances are right.

The correct view

For instance, introducing selflessness to someone who is dying might only scare them, so we must be careful.

Buddha Shakyamuni did not teach the final view to every student he encountered. He taught what was appropriate and suitable to their level. The teacher does not have free rein to teach whatever they choose. The students dictate what teachings are given. Since the teachings are meant to benefit the students, they must be tailored to their needs in accordance with their capacity.

In response to the second question, many people do have a negative self-image. In such cases we should speak to them about how meaningful and powerful our human bodies and minds can be. We can remind them that the potential of mind is unlimited and that, having obtained a human body, we can accomplish very meaningful things. The teachings on buddha potential demonstrate how far the mind can be developed, and this is only possible if we have the physical support of a human body. Not a dog or a cat or an elephant body, but a human body. It is a great mistake to think, 'I am worth nothing.' My acquaintances who work in hospices and as psychologists agree: when a person is having serious mental or emotional difficulties, we should try to help them appreciate the value of what they have — a human life. To teach a person selflessness while they are in crisis is not a good idea. The danger that they will misunderstand is too great.

Two truths

The Buddha taught two truths: ultimate truth and relative truth. Emptiness is ultimate truth. Phenomena other than emptiness are relative truths. Both are important and neither should be overlooked. In his *Introduction to the Middle Way*, the glorious Chandrakirti said that method and wisdom are the two wings that allow us to fly to the state of buddhahood.[2] Here, method refers to the methods that realise and make use of relative truths, while wisdom realises ultimate truths.

Ultimate truth refers only to emptiness, while renunciation, loving-kindness and compassion are relative truths. Relative truths are true according to the conventions of the world and are also called conventional truths. We must increase our familiarity with both ultimate and relative truths in order to attain buddhahood.

In verse eleven, Lama Tsongkhapa observes that a person has not realised Buddha Shakyamuni's intention if they find interdependence incompatible with emptiness. Yet many people wonder how a thing that does not inherently exist could exist at all. And how could an interdependent entity not exist inherently? Such qualms are, however, a sign that emptiness has not yet been understood. Emptiness and interdependence are not disparate. That is, they do not exist in isolation apart from one another; they are totally compatible and not exclusive.

Perhaps it would help to discuss the meaning of 'inherent existence'. Literally, something that exists inherently is established by nature. Yet if a thing were established by nature, in and of itself, its existence would not depend on other factors, which is untenable. Though phenomena are not *established by* nature they do *possess* a certain nature. These natures are defined by certain characteristics through which their identity is known. All phenomena 'retain their own entities' in the sense that a phenomenon is defined as this or that by the essence it holds. Think of a mug, for instance. How could we know what a mug is if there were no essence of what a mug is, or if a mug had no defining characteristics? Since a mug is, in essence, a container for drinks, generally with a certain shape, we know one when we see one.

So conventionally existent objects are defined by their essence or nature even if they are not established by them. Objects have a certain nature that allows us to distinguish them from other objects. But objects are not established by that nature because an object is established as such merely through being designated by names and conception. If a mug were established by nature and not established by name and conception we would never have to name or designate or define it — the thing would already be established as such. What's more, if a mug were established by its own characteristics and not by being designated by name and conception, we should be able to find the mug among its parts. But we can find no mug amid the bases for designating mug, only parts.

We use names and concepts to differentiate one object from another. For instance, 'vase' is a convention that designates those things that have flat bases and are capable of holding water and flowers. We arrive at this convention through consensus, isolating certain defining characteristics and giving them a name. Why is this significant? It demonstrates that things do not exist from their own side. Though things appear to exist inherently, they do not. They are established in dependence upon other factors.

Consider also the notions of 'friend' and 'foe'. If a person were established by nature or character as 'foe', they could never be anything but our enemy. That person would have been our foe from birth and could never become our 'friend'. The same applies to friends and strangers. Yet this is not how things are. We all know that a person becomes our friend or foe in dependence upon certain events and circumstances, among other things. Later, the person who was our friend becomes our enemy and vice versa. Recognising this helps us to understand that although it seems as if a person's very character established him or her as an enemy, that is not actually so. Failing to see this, we put stock in mistaken appearances and misleading perceptions, which in turn inflame anger and attachment.

The correct view

Phenomena are established through being designated by name and conception. As we discussed in Chapter 2, conceptual minds apprehend ideas and perceptual minds apprehend marks. Conceptual minds rely upon concepts, or generic images. A conceptual mind conjures up a generic image of the thing it thinks about to 'get at' that thing. For instance, when you think of your car an image of it comes to mind. This image is not your car but it represents your car in your thoughts. Perceptual minds are somewhat different in that they 'get at' their objects more directly, without the media of generic images. Yet they still discriminate between one object and another.

Think of an animal. Animals do not have the capacity for rational thought and language to the same extent that we humans do. They can communicate, but are much more limited in what they can express. So although a cow might not 'label' something 'good' or 'bad', it would still make the distinction. Its discrimination is linked to names and conceptions on some subtle level even if it does not verbally express it. These in turn are linked to the 'marks' that perceptual minds use to discriminate one thing from another. Conceptualisation is dependent on language. Language is dependent on conceptualisation. Which came first, the chicken or the egg? We cannot really say!

It may now seem obvious that interdependence and

emptiness are complementary and do not preclude one another. But actually to fully appreciate this is not so simple. Many masters have closely looked into this issue and found it difficult to maintain. Lama Tsongkhapa himself arrived at his understanding only after enduring years of hardship and study.

Based on what we know, we might say, 'It is easy to understand how a thing that exists interdependently cannot exist inherently.' But finding it so easy is not necessarily a good sign! Once we have reflected on this for a long while we will appreciate how difficult it is to overcome all doubts and fully reconcile the two truths. Older teachers used to say to us, 'Saying "I understand" is a sign that you do not. Saying "I just cannot seem to grasp this point" is a sign that you understand a bit.' My teacher, who was an abbot of Sera Je Monastery, often asked us, 'Do you understand?' If someone said 'Yes!' he would slowly shake his head and say, 'I doubt you do.' So no one dared open their mouth when asked; we would all look down to avoid his glance!

The simultaneity of the two truths

Once emptiness and interdependence have been properly understood, the thought of the one naturally leads to thoughts of the other. We have not completed our analysis of the view until this point. Verse twelve reads:

The correct view

At some point in time, suddenly, they cease to alternate
And just by seeing that interdependence is unfailing
A certainty that destroys all misapprehensions comes about.
At that time your analysis of the view is complete.

Ideally the thought of emptiness follows on from all of our meditations. For instance, when cultivating the mind of enlightenment we should recognise that we, the meditators, are empty of inherent existence, just as the enlightenment we seek and those for whom we seek it are too. Before we perceptually realise emptiness we must understand the emptiness of the agent, object and action: the three spheres.

To realise emptiness — lack of inherent existence — we must understand what it means for something to inherently exist. We must recognise how the misapprehensions of self, which apprehend inherently existent things, are wrong. If a thing existed inherently, it would exist independent of causes and conditions, parts and/or a basis of designation. In other words, inherent existence precludes dependent existence, and vice versa. Realising interdependence then undermines the misapprehension of self until finally we no longer conceive of inherently existent phenomena. The misconception cannot remain in the face of a deep realisation of dependent arising.

If a horse trainer sees that an animal has horns, he or

she will recognise that it is not a horse. Likewise, a person who understands dependent arising will recognise that things do not exist inherently; the apprehension of dependent existence contradicts the misapprehension of inherent existence.

The thirteenth verse reads:

> *Furthermore, appearances clear away the extreme of*
> *existence and*
> *Emptiness clears away the extreme of non-existence.*
> *When you understand how emptiness shows itself as cause*
> *and result*
> *You can never be held captive by extreme views.*

There are many different schools of philosophy within Buddhism, such as the Great Exposition school and the Sutra school. Even with the Mahayana, there are different schools such as the Mind Only school, the Middle Way Autonomist school and the Middle Way Consequence school. Yet only the Middle Way Consequence school teaches the final view: that appearances clear away the extreme of existence and that emptiness clears away the extreme of non-existence.

The more common explanation, and in some ways more expected, holds that appearances clear away the extreme of non-existence — nihilism — and emptiness clears away the extreme of existence — eternalism. The appearance of phenomena proves that they exist, dispelling nihilistic notions. That they are empty of inherent existence proves that they do not exist inherently, dispelling eternalistic ideas.

Lama Tsongkhapa alters the formula to say that appearances dispel the extreme of eternalistic existence and emptiness dispels the extreme of nihilistic non-existence. In doing so he calls attention to the inseparability of interdependence and emptiness.

'Appearances' refer to conventional phenomena, relative truths that appear to our mind and senses. Anything that appears — assuming that it exists — is established in dependence upon and in relation to other things. Merely by appearing, they prove that they do not exist inherently; how could anything independent of all else appear? It could not, so appearances clear away the extreme of existence.

Emptiness is common to everything that exists because all phenomena are empty of inherent existence. Any given emptiness depends upon the subject that is the basis for it. Yet the fact that emptiness is the final nature of all phenomena does not mean that phenomena do not exist, as many would think. Quite the contrary, in fact. A thing that inherently existed would be non-existent; to exist inherently is to not exist! But phenomena are empty of inherent existence and established in dependence upon causes, parts or bases of designation. Emptiness clears away the extreme of non-existence.

Emptiness can be understood by considering the way causes produce effects. The infallibility of cause and effect can be understood through emptiness. If phenomena arise interdependently they cannot exist inherently. If phenomena exist, but not inherently, they must exist interdependently.

We can train in emptiness so that the mere appearance of conventional objects causes the notion of emptiness to arise in our mind. The thought of emptiness can in turn engender thoughts of dependent arising. Gradually the misapprehension of self — the root of all disturbing emotions — weakens as the object it conceives is destroyed.

Meditating on emptiness helps us to develop wisdom, but it can also make us more kind-hearted. We are now only beginners and our renunciation and minds of enlightenment are in their earliest stages. Yet we still want our efforts to have a positive impact on our lives. How can this be done?

We consistently overestimate the elements of our experience: the self, others, our bodies, objects. We assume that they exist as they appear to us. We make judgements — good, bad, pleasant, unpleasant — and react strongly with attachment and anger. What gives these disturbing emotions their strength? The fact that we hold the people and objects we are attached to or angry at to exist as they appear. These misapprehensions initially generate disturbing emotions and later inflame them. If we recognise that appearances are interdependent and are not established from their own side, the grasping becomes weaker. If we understand that things are merely imputed by name and conception, would disturbing emotions have such a firm basis? If we destroy their foundation we destroy disturbing emotions. To destroy their foundation we must find the remedy and apply an antidote to the misapprehension of self.

An intellectual understanding of emptiness is not enough. Emptiness must be realised. And once it is realised, we need to familiarise ourselves with the realisation. This is the meaning of the fourteenth verse, which reads:

> *When you realise as I have the crux*
> *Of the three principal aspects of the path explained here,*
> *Then, my child, stay in isolation, persevere with joy and*
> *Quickly accomplish the perfect goal that lies ahead.*

Seclusion

After giving these teachings, Lama Tsongkhapa advised his students, and by extension us, to seek isolation or seclusion, once we have developed renunciation, the mind of enlightenment and the correct view.

Isolation is of two types: external and internal. External isolation refers to being isolated from commotion and the hustle-bustle of life, symbolised by the marketplace. Internal isolation refers to isolating, or separating, our mind from disturbing emotions. Isolating ourself from external things will do no good if we cannot isolate our mind from disturbing emotions. Without internal isolation we will not truly be isolated, even if we live in remote, unpopulated mountains; in fact, there is the danger that we will go crazy! Yet if we isolate our mind from disturbing emotions and misconceptions, commotion will have no detrimental effect.

Should misconceptions and disturbing emotions arise, we must not leave them be; we must apply their antidote straight away. As Geshe Langri Tangpa says in his *Eight Verses on Training the Mind*, 'May I overcome these belligerent disturbing emotions, harmful to me and others, as soon as they arise.' Do not wait for them to arise. Try to block any opportunity they have to arise. Remember that there are two ways to deal with disturbing emotions. The first approach concentrates on developing equanimity, loving-kindness and compassion. These are immediate measures to stop disturbing emotions from manifesting. The second approach focuses on emptiness: developing the antidote to the misapprehensions that lie at the root of disturbing emotions, so as to destroy them and their seeds.

We should use our capacity for logic and reasoning to develop the mind in a positive way. Examination for examination's sake has its limitations. We must also understand how the conclusions that we reach are relevant to our practice. There is a fault in not relating it back to our practice. We do not have the same aims as scientists. Our primary concern is not material development. We seek to develop the mind and its positive potential so we must not lose sight of the purpose of our inquiries. Our studies and training should help us to recognise our exaggerations and errors. They should help us become better people.

8

Working with the mind

This concluding chapter discusses the importance of working with the mind. By working with the mind we can understand the way it dictates our actions and the way our actions determine our experiences. As all beings want to be happy and do not want to suffer, these truths transcend religion. These truths can be and ought to be applied by all people. From the sincere application of these truths springs a kinder, gentler heart and a more tolerant mind.

What is the heart of Buddhism?

The heart of Buddhism is to develop a good heart; to develop and improve our minds. Lama Tsongkhapa said, 'If the intention is good, the grounds and paths will be good. If the intention is bad, the grounds and path will be bad.' In other words, everything depends upon the mind. The paths that we follow are determined by the state of our mind, be this positive or negative. Some people have it relatively easy; they enjoy a nice, comfortable life. Others have more difficulties. If you were to choose ten people, you would find that none live the same life: an enormous number of variables make the life of one person different from that of another. According to Buddhism, this is due to the mind and past actions.

The Buddha's teachings can be encapsulated in this famous verse from a sutra:

> *To commit not a single negativity,*
> *To perform a wealth of wholesome acts,*
> *To subdue our minds —*
> *This is the teaching of the Buddha.*

Negative states of mind lead to negative acts; positive states of mind lead to wholesome acts. Suffering is the result of negative acts, and happiness is the result of wholesome acts. Subduing the mind encourages the one and pacifies the other.

The Buddha did not issue commands to us. He appealed to our own sense of reason and discrimination. Understanding the mind and the relationship between actions and their effects, we conclude that we ought to develop goodwill and embrace wholesome acts, and discard ill will and refrain from negative acts. We know this is in our own best interests and the interests of others. As it is true for us, it is true of others.

Buddhists pray, 'May all sentient beings be happy,' not 'May Buddhists be happy.' If a person is genuinely concerned with the happiness of others, their primary concern is not with converting people to Buddhism. We must consider other individuals and how we can bring them happiness in a way that is appropriate to them and their situation. Some sentient beings will not be inclined towards Buddhism and some may not like it at all. Would pushing Buddhism on them make them happy? It would be unskilful to adopt that approach. We wish for the happiness of all beings regardless of their religious or secular affiliation. Therefore, we must work for the happiness of others while respecting their differences.

It is my hope that this book greatly benefits its readers; this is my sole motivation in teaching Buddhism. But remember, a mere understanding will give you only so much. To derive maximum benefit from these teachings they must be applied in our lives. If you can do this, I have no doubt you will find this book helpful. When reading a book or listening to teachings on Buddhism, we ought to examine what we read and hear in light of our own experiences. By comparing our experiences with the teachings we receive, we can separate the good from the bad and develop our minds. This is of utmost importance.

What do we mean when we speak of 'developing the mind'? We mean to decrease the duration and strength of disturbing emotions that taint the mind and increase the duration and strength of positive states. Quite simply, it means to eliminate disturbing emotions and encourage positive states of mind. When we do so, our mind begins to resemble the positive and is dissociated from the negative.

Meditation is this very process: developing the mind. To meditate on loving-kindness and compassion means to cultivate loving-kindness and compassion. To do this, we must arouse a sense of loving-kindness and compassion. We must let the mind become acquainted with positive states. In doing so we eliminate the opportunities where anger, envy and other negative states of mind can arise.

It is our responsibility to make such changes. If ever there was work to do, this is certainly it!

Glossary

Abhidharma   Abhidharma is one of the five major subjects of the Tibetan monastic curriculum. This subject is based on the sutras included in the third of three collections, the Abhidharma collection, or 'collection of manifest knowledge'. There are two systems of Abhidharma, explained by the brothers Vasubandhu and Asanga respectively. Vasubandhu's *Treasury of the Abhidharma* presents the collection of manifest knowledge from the perspective of the two lower schools of Buddhist philosophy: the Great Exposition school and the Sutra school. Asanga's *Compendium of Abhidharma* presents the material from the Mahayana perspective. The emphasis of the Abhidharma literature is on developing the training in wisdom.

aggregates   Basically, aggregates are the physical and mental components of our existence. There is one physical aggregate, the aggregate of form, and there are four mental ones. Our bodies are aggregates of form, while mind, feeling, discrimination and composition are the four mental aggregates.

analytical meditation   Generally there are two types of meditation: analytical and placement. Analytical meditation uses reasons and logic to develop wisdom about a topic. Meditations on loving-kindness and compassion are considered 'analytical' because they involve thinking about their nature, focus, aspect, advantages and what they overcome.

arhat An arhat is a person who attained liberation by abandoning disturbing emotions and their seeds. Arhats are followers of the hearer or solitary realiser paths.

Arya Buddha An Arya Buddha is a person who has attained buddhahood. Such a person has developed the qualities of wisdom, compassion and ability to their utmost extent by abandoning emotional and cognitive obscurations.

Aryadeva Aryadeva was a second- to third-century disciple of the Middle Way pioneer, Nagarjuna. He composed a famous text entitled *Four Hundred Verses on the Middle Way*.

Asanga The noble Asanga (fifth century CE), or Arya Asanga as he is more commonly known, is an important figure in the lineage of teachings on the bodhisattva paths and conduct. After receiving the *Five Dharmas of Maitreya* directly from the Lord Maitreyanatha, he introduced them to the world. Among these texts are *The Ornament of Clear Realisation* and *Sublime Continuum*.

Atisha Atisha (982–1054 CE) was an important Indian scholar who composed the first systematic presentation of the stages of the path, or lam rim. He is regarded as founder of the Kadampa school, which had a strong influence on what became the Gelug school.

bodhicitta Bodhicitta is a Sanskrit term that means 'mind of enlightenment'. It is a mind that strives to attain enlightenment in order to free all sentient beings from suffering. As a 'gateway into the Mahayana paths' it is central to a bodhisattva's practice.

Glossary

bodhisattva   A bodhisattva is a person who has developed an uncontrived mind of enlightenment.

bodhisattva grounds   There are ten bodhisattva grounds that a bodhisattva passes through as they progress through the Mahayana paths of seeing and meditation. A bodhisattva's qualities increase as they attain each successive ground until eventually all positive qualities are developed to their utmost extent and the bodhisattva becomes a buddha.

Buddha   Buddha is one of Buddhism's Three Jewels of Refuge. The term 'buddha' may refer to a person, like the historical Shakyamuni Buddha, but it may also refer to the omniscience of such a person. The Sanskrit term 'buddha' means 'enlightened' or 'awakened one'. This is rendered into Tibetan as *sangs rgyas*, which roughly means 'cleansed and developed'.

Buddha Shakyamuni   Buddha Shakyamuni is the founder of Buddhism who lived around the Gangetic plain of north-central India during the fifth century BCE. He was born Siddhartha Gautama, a prince of the Shakya clan whose kingdom was located in parts of present-day Nepal and India. At the age of twenty-nine he left home in the hope of finding a way to end suffering. He mastered the doctrines taught by well-known teachers of the day, yet was not convinced that he had found a path to liberation. After six years he was convinced that the path to freedom lay neither in the extreme of asceticism nor in the extreme of indulgent hedonism. He then manifested enlightenment under a tree in Bodh Gaya, now in the Indian state of Bihar, and went on to teach the Middle Way for forty-five years.

buddhahood   A state of consummate wisdom, compassion and ability in which all emotional and cognitive obscurations have been completely removed.

calm abiding   Calm abiding is a state of meditative absorption in which a person can place their attention on an object in whichever way they please. It is infused with the bliss that comes from having overcome negative habitual tendencies and developed a totally pliant body and mind.

cause and effect   Cause and effect occurs both internally and externally. Internal cause and effect refers to karma and its effects (see *karma*), while external cause and effect refers to the causal process we witness in the environment around us. Though the sphere of activity differs, both internal and external cause and effect operate on the same basic principle: that all effects arise from causes of a similar type. For instance, a mango seed produces a mango tree not an orange tree; the seed of a positive action produces a positive effect not a negative one.

Chandrakirti   Chandrakirti (540–600 CE) was a great Indian master from Nalanda Monastery who explained Nagarjuna's thought in famous works like *Introduction to the Middle Way* and *Clear Words*. He defended the master Buddhapalita's understanding of Nagarjuna's *The Fundamental Wisdom of the Middle Way* against Buddhapalita's critiques and in the process pioneered the Middle Way Consequence school.

contaminated   Technically, something that inflames the disturbing emotions or increases 'contamination' when a person focuses on it or possesses it.

cyclic existence Cyclic existence, or samsara, is the continual and repeated perpetuation of contaminated body and mind, a process propelled by karma and disturbing emotions.

Dalai Lama, His Holiness The present Dalai Lama, Tenzin Gyatso (1935– CE), is the Fourteenth in a succession of incarnate masters stretching back to Gedun Drub (1391–1471 CE), a student of Lama Tsongkhapa, the founder of the Gelug tradition. (See Robert Thurman's *Life and Teaching of Tsong Khapa*, Library of Tibetan Works and Archives, Dharamsala, 1982, p. 26.) Initially, the office of Dalai Lama was a purely religious position. But in 1642, a Mongol chieftain, Gushri Khan, invested the Fifth Dalai Lama, Ngawang Lozang Gyatso (1617–1682 CE), with political authority over Tibet. (See T. Shakaba, *Tibet, A Political History*, Potala, New York, 1984, p. 88.) From that time to 1959, the Dalai Lamas acted as both spiritual and temporal head of Tibet. Though nominally belonging to the Gelug school, all schools of Tibetan Buddhism revere the Dalai Lama.

Dharma Dharma is a Sanskrit word with many meanings. Here it is used to refer to the Buddha's teachings.

dharmakayas Every buddha has four *kayas*, or bodies. Two of these are dharmakayas, or reality bodies, and two are rupakayas, or form bodies. The first dharmakaya is the primordial awareness dharmakaya. This is a buddha's omniscient mind, which perceptually realises the empty nature of all things as well as things in all their diversity. The second dharmakaya is the essential body. This is the suchness of a buddha's mind, which is free of both emotional and cognitive obscurations.

Dharmakirti Dharmakirti (600–660 CE) was a seventh-century Indian master and heir to Dignaga's (480–540 CE) tradition of logic and epistemology. Dharmakirti wrote *A Commentary on Valid Cognition*, in which he explained how all valid knowledge is based on either perception or inference. This work has been the basis for studies of logic and epistemology in the Tibetan tradition to this day.

eight mundane concerns The eight mundane concerns taint the purity of a person's motivation. They include four pairs of opposites that involve an undue concern with gain, no gain, pleasure, pain, pleasant words, unpleasant words, praise and abuse. Such mundane concerns create emotional fluctuations that disturb a person's peace of mind. Like a boat battered by the ocean's waves, being pleased when one is praised and displeased when one is verbally abused causes a person to sink from elevated emotional highs to deflated emotional lows.

emptiness Emptiness is the ultimate nature of everything that exists. Nothing exists inherently; all phenomena are empty of inherent existence. The quality of 'being empty of inherent existence' is emptiness. This subtle mode of being is common to everything that exists and is considered to be ultimate truth. Emptiness is closely related to interdependence: things do not exist inherently because they exist interdependently.

enlightenment Generally, enlightenment refers to the 'great enlightenment', which is equivalent to buddhahood. In Sanskrit, enlightenment is *bodhi*, which implies awakening, for example, from the sleep of ignorance into the light of

Glossary

omniscience. In Tibetan, enlightenment is *byang chub*, which roughly translates as 'purified and perfected'. To attain enlightenment, a person must purify all stains and perfect all positive qualities.

equalising and exchanging self for others   This is one of two techniques used to develop a mind of enlightenment. This technique engenders loving-kindness and compassion by developing equanimity and reflecting on the shortcomings of self-cherishing and the benefits of cherishing others.

Four Noble Truths   Shakyamuni Buddha taught the Four Noble Truths in the first teaching he gave after his enlightenment. Shakyamuni advised that we should understand true suffering, abandon the true origins of suffering, actualise the true cessation of suffering and cultivate the true paths that free us from suffering. Hence, the Four Noble Truths teach that the unpleasant aspects of our existence have causes. If the causes can be found, they can be eliminated and we will be free from their unpleasant effects.

Ganden Monastery   In 1410, the Lord Tsongkhapa founded Ganden Monastery outside Lhasa in central Tibet. This monastic seat was the birthplace of the Gelug school, with its first three throne-holders being Tsongkhapa and his two spiritual sons, Gyaltshab Je (1364–1432 CE) and Khedrup Je (1385–1438 CE). Traditionally, the Ganden throne-holder is considered the supreme head of the Gelug school.

Gelug   The Gelug school first emerged at Ganden Monastery during the fifteenth century. The newest of the four schools of Tibetan Buddhism, this school traces its lineages back to Ganden's founder, Lama Tsongkhapa, who studied with teachers from many different traditions including the Sakya, Nyingma, and Kagyu. The Gelug are often regarded as heirs to Atisha's famed Kadam school. The Gelug school is renowned for the high quality of its scholars and the value it places on the monastic lifestyle.

Hinayana The Hinayana tradition is a generic name applied to the hearer and solitary realiser vehicles of Buddhism. The hearer vehicle includes the eighteen schools of early Indian Buddhism. Of those only the Theravadin tradition remains today. Generally, practitioners of the solitary realiser vehicle live in seclusion and do not rely on teachers. They prefer to tread a solitary path, hence the name. The goal of a Hinayana practitioner is to attain liberation from suffering and its causes, and thus their greatest fear is becoming attached to the pleasures of cyclic existence.

inherent existence Inherent existence is what emptiness negates. According to the Middle Way Consequence school it is interchangeable with true existence and existence from one's own side. To inherently exist implies that a thing exists independent of all other things. Since everything exists in dependence upon other things, be they causes, parts or a basis for imputation, nothing inherently exists.

insight Insight is a form of analytical meditation employed once calm abiding has been achieved. Insight into the object of meditation increases the bliss and stability attained in calm abiding.

Glossary

Kachen Yeshe Gyaltshan   Kachen Yeshe Gyaltshan (1713–1793 CE) was tutor to the Eighth Dalai Lama and author of many works important to the Gelug tradition.

Kagyu   The Kagyu school traces its lineages back to Marpa the Translator (1012–1097 CE) who was a student of the great Indian yogis Naropa and Maitripa. What we know as the Kagyu school is not a single unified tradition but a conglomeration of many traditions that trace their lineages to roughly the same source. It is common to speak of the four main schools and eight sub-schools of the Kagyu, but this does not take all Kagyu lineages into account. The Kagyu lineages enjoy a reputation as 'practice lineages' due to the great emphasis they place on Mahamudra, the Six Yogas and long meditation retreats.

karma   Karma is a Sanskrit term that means 'action'. Thus, the word 'karma' implies activity, of body and speech; but, most importantly, of mind. Karma refers to the intentional mental activity that accompanies every act. Since every act is accompanied by mental activity, every act imbues the mind with a certain potential, which is called a karmic seed, and leaves an impression on the mind, which is called a karmic imprint. Karmic seeds have the potential to produce either a pleasant or unpleasant effect, while karmic imprints predispose the mind towards certain things. It is important to distinguish between karma, which is intentional mental activity, and karmic seeds and imprints, which are products of karma.

lam rim   The lam rim, or stages of the path, is a literary genre begun by Atisha's *A Lamp for the Path to Enlightenment*.

Typically, lam rim texts begin with the way to rely upon a spiritual teacher and end with a discussion of Tantra. In the process they unify and systematically present the paths that lead to favourable rebirths, liberation and buddhahood. The lam rim is sometimes called the 'graduated path', a phrase that belies its sequential structure.

Lam Rim Chenmo The *Lam Rim Chenmo*, or *The Great Treatise on the Stages of the Path to Enlightenment*, is an extensive work on the path to enlightenment written by Lama Tsongkhapa. In it, he distinguishes between three orientations: beings of small scope aim for higher status rebirths; beings of middling scope aim for liberation; while beings of great scope aim for buddhahood. Accordingly, there are certain stages of the path that an individual must cultivate to attain their respective goal. This work is widely considered a masterpiece and is revered in the tradition for its clarity and the numerous scriptural citations it contains.

Lamp for the Path to Enlightenment, A This text by Atisha is the first proper lam rim text. It was composed specifically for the Tibetans, who found the extensive Indian Buddhist tradition hard to grasp. Presented in verse, the text addresses the essentials of the Sutra path. Hugely successful, it became the model for texts by masters of all four Tibetan Buddhist schools.

Lhasa Lhasa is the capital of Tibet. It is located in the province of U, or central Tibet.

Mahayana The Mahayana is a name given to the bodhisattva vehicle. The goal of a Mahayanist is to attain buddhahood for the sake of all sentient beings. The Mahayana places great emphasis on cherishing others and overcoming selfishness. More than anything a Mahayanist fears falling prey to the type of self-interest that makes a person indifferent to the plight of others.

Maitreya Maitreya, whose name means 'One of loving kindness', is Buddha Shakyamuni's regent. He resides in Tushita heaven, where he taught Asanga the *Five Dharmas of Maitreya*, and will eventually come to Earth as the fifth (of one thousand) Buddha of this aeon.

Maitripa Maitripa was one of the Eighty-four Mahasiddhas or greatly accomplished yogis of India.

mani A Sanskrit word meaning 'jewel'. It is one of the main words in the Compassion Buddha's mantra.

Manjushri Like Maitreya, Manjushri is listed as one of the eight close sons of Shakyamuni in the Mahayana sutras. He is considered an embodiment of buddha wisdom and is associated with their speech. Often referred to as a bodhisattva, Manjushri will appear as the sixth Buddha of this aeon.

Mantra The Mantra vehicle, or Tantra as it is often called in the West, is part of the larger Mahayana vehicle. It includes a body of techniques such as visualisation of deities and recitation of mantras, which allow a practitioner to remove emotional and cognitive obscurations and attain buddhahood quickly.

Marpa Marpa the Translator (1012–1097 CE) travelled many times to India and studied under the two great Indian yogis Naropa and Maitripa. Eventually he returned to Tibet for good, where he passed on these teachings to students like Milarepa and founded the Kagyu tradition.

meditative equipoise Meditative equipoise is a balanced and even state in which a person focuses one-pointedly on an object of meditation.

Middle Way Consequence school The Middle Way Consequence school is one of two Middle Way schools. There was no unified movement in India that corresponds to what we call the Middle Way Consequence school; rather, it is a name coined by later Tibetan authors to distinguish Chandrakirti's interpretation of Nagarjuna's work from Bhavya's. It is widely considered to be the 'highest' school of Buddhist tenets. Proponents of this school maintain that logical consequences are the best way to establish the correct view in debate, and thus the name.

Middle Way philosophy In his commentaries on *The Perfection of Wisdom Sutras*, Nagarjuna pioneered the Middle Way philosophy, which is considered the highest of four Buddhist tenet schools. In explaining ultimate and relative truth, this school treads the middle way between the two extremes of nihilism and eternalism. In asserting the emptiness of all phenomena, it avoids the realist philosophy of the Hinayana schools and the idealist philosophy of the Mind Only school.

Milarepa Milarepa (1040–1123 CE) was a student of Marpa and a great saint of the Kagyu tradition. As a youth he harmed many people, but later developed great regret for his misdeeds and went on to become a highly accomplished yogi. He is an example of how strong dedication to the spiritual path can lead to quick and profound results.

Nagarjuna Nagarjuna was an early and extremely important figure in the development of the Mahayana. He lived in the first centuries of the Christian era. He is said to have retrieved *The Perfection of Wisdom Sutras* from their traditional caretakers and introduced them to the world. He wrote many original works, like *The Fundamental Wisdom of the Middle Way*, which clarified the intention of the sutras of the middle turning. In the process he pioneered the first Mahayana tenet school, the Middle Way.

Naropa One of the Eighty-four Mahasiddhas and the principal guru of Marpa the Translator.

nirvana Nirvana means 'passed beyond sorrow'. It is the abandonment of emotional obscurations — that is, disturbing emotions and their seeds. Having attained it, a person enjoys unchanging pleasure but has not yet abandoned cognitive obscurations. A person does not perfect wisdom or ability merely by attaining nirvana, so a bodhisattva aims higher, namely for the great enlightenment of buddhahood.

Nyingma The Nyingma school of Tibetan Buddhism traces its lineages back to the Indian masters Guru Rinpoche and Shantarakshita, important figures in Buddhism's introduction to Tibet. Though this tradition has produced many notable scholars, such as Rongzom Pandita, Longchenpa and Ju Mipham Rinpoche, the Nyingma are more commonly associated with the teachings of Mantra and Dzogchen, in particular.

pandita   Pandita is a Sanskrit word meaning 'learned' or 'expert'. The English word 'pundit' is a corruption of pandita. In India this was a title used by Buddhists and non-Buddhists alike to indicate a person's mastery of a religious system, medicine, music or other traditional bodies of knowledge.

Phurbu Chog   The tutor Phurbu Chog Jampa Tsultrim Gyatso (1825–1901 CE) was a well-known Gelug master and author of several texts on collected topics.

placement meditation   Whereas analytical meditation uses reason and analysis to understand a topic, placement meditation dwells one-pointedly on what has been understood. Analytical meditations may consider many points related to a single topic, while placement meditations generally focus only on a single thing.

refuge   Buddhists seek refuge from suffering and its causes. The actual refuge is the Three Dharma Jewels. Actualising a Dharma Jewel protects a person from suffering and its causes. The Buddha Jewel teaches refuge, while the Sangha Jewel helps others to achieve it.

rupakayas   The rupakayas, or form bodies, are the two buddha bodies that a person achieves for the sake of others. The two rupakayas are the *sambhogakaya*, or enjoyment body, and the *nirmanakaya*, or emanation body. The enjoyment body abides in the realm of Akanishtha, teaching the Mahayana to a retinue of noble bodhisattvas. The emanation body may take a variety of forms, all of which are intended to help sentient beings become free of suffering.

Sakya   The Sakya tradition traces its lineages back to the great Indian yogi Virupa. After bringing his teachings to Tibet, the translator Drokmi established the Sakya school in central Tibet, promoting the famous 'Path and Fruit' system. This school is renowned for its vigorous tradition of learning, and masters of all traditions, including Tsongkhapa, have trained in Sakya institutions. A lively rivalry between Sakya and Gelug masters has developed over the years, covering both major and minor points of doctrine.

samsara   Samsara, or cyclic existence, literally means 'a cycle'. See 'cyclic existence'.

Sanskrit   Sanskrit, an Indo-European language, was to ancient and medieval India what Latin was to medieval Europe. The Mahayana sutras, as well as Brahmanical texts like the Vedas, were written in Sanskrit.

sentient being   Beings are either buddhas or sentient beings. A sentient being is a being whose mind is still subject to emotional and/or cognitive obscurations. Buddhas are free of both.

sevenfold instruction on causes and effect   The sevenfold instruction on causes and effect is a method for developing the mind of enlightenment that Maitreya taught to Asanga. By cultivating six causes — knowing all sentient beings have been one's mother, remembering their kindness, wishing to repay that kindness, loving-kindness, compassion and the highest intention — the mind of enlightenment arises as their effect. It is also known as the 'six causes and one result'.

shastra Shastra is a Sanskrit word meaning 'treatise'. Indian Buddhist literature is divided into sutras and shastras. Sutras are understood to be the word of Buddha Shakyamuni while shastras are commentaries composed by other Indian Buddhist masters.

six perfections, the The six perfections are the perfection of: generosity, ethics, patience, joyous effort, concentration and wisdom. Mahayanists practise the six perfections as a way to help others and as a way to gather the two collections of merit and wisdom.

stupa A stupa is a reliquary where relics of past masters or holy objects are placed. A consecrated stupa is thus an object of veneration and a symbol of buddha mind.

Sublime Continuum, The *The Sublime Continuum* is one of the *Five Dharmas of Maitreya* the Lord Maitreya taught to the noble Asanga. It is one of the main Indian commentaries on buddha potential.

suchness A synonym for emptiness.

sutra Sutras are discourses given or presided over by Shakyamuni Buddha. The Buddhist canon has two parts: the sutras and shastras. While sutras are generally taken to be the word of Buddha, the shastras are treatises commenting on those written by later Indian masters.

Three Scopes, the The Three Scopes are a way to classify beings according to their orientations and aims. See *Lam Rim Chenmo*.

Glossary

Tsongkhapa, Lama   As a youth, Lama Tsongkhapa (1357–1419 CE) came from the north-eastern province of Tibet, Amdo, to study with the great masters of central Tibet. He studied ecumenically, completing his education in the major subjects of Buddhism under some of the most prestigious teachers of his day. In 1409, he initiated the Great Prayer Festival in Lhasa and a year later founded Ganden Monastery, where he continued to teach until his death in 1419. His students, particularly Gyaltshab Je, Khedrup Je and the First Dalai Lama Gendun Drub, spread the Ganden tradition to other parts of Tibet until it was established as one of the four major schools of Tibetan Buddhism. Tsongkhapa was a prolific writer, composing many texts in a clear, eloquent and logical style.

Two Truths, the   The Two Truths are ultimate truth and relative truth. Briefly, ultimate truth is emptiness, while relative truth includes everything else that exists. Relative truths, like 'chair' or 'mountain', exist conventionally, but when analysed cannot be found. There is thus a discrepancy between the way they exist and the way they appear. When perceptually realised, there is no such discrepancy with ultimate truth, emptiness.

Vasubandhu   Vasubandhu (400–480 CE), brother of Asanga, summarised the Abhidharma system according to the hearer vehicle in his great text *Treasury of the Abhidharma*. He wrote many important texts like *The Ornament of Sutra* and *Distinguishing the Middle from the Extremes*.

Vinaya   Vinaya refers to the ethics of individual liberation as taught by Shakyamuni Buddha. Through anecdote and story, the Buddha gave guidelines on how to live ethically. Thus the Vinaya details the vows and proscriptions that frame the lives of monks and nuns.

Yamantaka   Yamantaka is a Highest Yoga Tantra deity, considered to be the wrathful emanation of Manjushri.

Notes

Chapter 2
1. *An Explanation of Subject and Object* by Phurbu Chog.
2. *The Precious Garland* [Skt *Ratnavali*, Tib. *rin chen phreng ba*] by Nagarjuna, c. second century CE.
3. *The Compendium of Knowledge* [Skt *Abhidharma-samuccaya*, Tib. *chos mngon pa kun btus*] by Arya Asanga, mid fifth century CE.

Chapter 3
1. *The Sublime Continuum* [Skt *Uttaratantra*, Tib. *rgyud bla ma*] by Maitreya, as recorded by Asanga, mid fifth century CE, is one of the *Five Dharmas of Maitreya*.
2. ibid.
3. The ten bodhisattva grounds are ten stages a bodhisattva passes through on the way to attaining buddhahood. Progress is accompanied by an increase in one's positive qualities and an increased familiarity with one's perceptual realisation of emptiness.
4. *Sutra on the Ten Grounds* [Skt *dashabhumika sutra*, Tib. *sa bchu'i mdo*] by Shakyamuni Buddha.

Chapter 5
1. Verse 29, page 30, as quoted in *bshes pa'i springs yig gi rnam bshad 'phags pa' dgongs pa kun gsal. A Letter to a Friend* [Skt *Suhrlleka*, Tib. *bshes springs yig*], was originally a letter Nagarjuna wrote to his friend, the King Good Conduct of Happiness [*bDe spyod bzang po*] on how to live a good and meaningful life. Since Nagarjuna's advice is applicable to all of us and not just the king, it has become a popular text in the Tibetan tradition. Translation here is by Lozang Zopa. The entire work, together with a commentary, has been translated into English by Geshe Lobsang Tharchin and Artemus B. Engle under the title *Nagarjuna's Letter*, Library of Tibetan Works and Archives, Dharamsala, 1979.

Chapter 7
1. *In Praise of Dependent Arising* [Tib. *rten 'brel bstod pa*] by Tsongkhapa, 1357–1419.

2   *Introduction to the Middle Way* [Skt *Madhyamaka-avatara*, Tib. *dbu ma la 'jug pa*] by Chandrakirti. This is a commentary and supplement to Nagarjuna's *The Fundamental Wisdom of the Middle Way* [Skt *prajna nama mula madhyamaka karika*, Tib. *dbu ma rtsa ba'i tshig leur byas pa shes rab*].

Recommended reading

General
The Dalai Lama, *The World of Tibetan Buddhism: An Overview of its Philosophy and Practice*, trans. and ed. by Geshe Thubten Jinpa, Wisdom Publications, Boston, 1995.
The Dalai Lama and Howard C. Cutler, *The Art of Happiness*, Hodder Headline, Sydney, 1998.
Lafitte, Gabriel, and Ribush, Alison, *Happiness in a Material World: The Dalai Lama in Australia and New Zealand*, Lothian Books, Melbourne, 2002.
McDonald, Kathleen, *How to Meditate: A Practical Guide*, Wisdom Publications, Boston, 1995.

Mind
Rabten, Geshe, *Mind and Its Functions*, Rabten Edition, 1992.

Buddha potential
Loden, Geshe Thubten, *Fundamental Potential for Enlightenment*, Tushita Publications, Melbourne, 1996.

History and overview of Tibetan Buddhism and Gelug tradition
Thurman, Robert A. F., *Essential Tibetan Buddhism*, HarperCollins, San Francisco, 1996.

Mind of enlightenment
Shantideva, *Guide to the Bodhisattva's Way of Life*, Library of Tibetan Works and Archives, Dharamsala, 1982.
Rinchen, Geshe Sonam, *The Bodhisattva Vow*, trans. Ruth Sonam, Snow Lion, Ithaca, 2000.

Correct view of emptiness
The Dalai Lama, *Essence of the Heart Sutra*, trans. and ed. by Geshe Thubten Jinpa, Wisdom Publications, Boston, 2002.

Index

Abhidharma 85, 245, 261
aggregates 112, 245
arhat 117–18, 246
  differences with a buddha 167–8
Aryadeva 20–1, 246
  Four Hundred Verses on the Middle Way 246
Asanga 245, 246, 255, 261
  Compendium of Knowledge 29, 245, 263
Atisha 246
  the life of 79–83
  A Lamp for the Path to Enlightenment 79, 82, 253, 254
attachment 120–4, 175
beings of the three scopes 92–3, 260
Bodhicitta 51, 64, 159–60, 246
  contrived and uncontrived 64–5
  generating 162–4
  highest intention 51–2, 160, 189
bodhisattva 52, 247
bodhisattva grounds 57, 247, 263
Buddha 61, 114
  nature of 38
buddha bodies
  dharma bodies (see *dharmakaya*)
  form bodies (see *rupakaya*)
buddha nature 36
  awakening 60–4
  naturally present potential 36
  potential for buddhahood 36, 42, 71
buddha potential (see *buddha nature*)
buddhahood 105, 165, 247
  need for 190
cause and effect 8, 140–2, 218, 248
  substantial causes 140
Chandrakirti 21, 187, 248
  Introduction to the Middle Way 226, 248, 264
  Clear Words 248
contaminated pleasures 50
cyclic existence 20, 111–12, 121–2, 171–2, 249
Dalai Lama, His Holiness the 78, 224, 249

death (certainty of; uncertainty of time) 127–33
Dharma 7, 64, 110, 129, 153, 249
dharmakaya 45, 249
Dharmakirti 250
  A Commentary on Valid Cognition 250
  Seven Treatises on Valid Cognition 84
disturbing emotions 7, 20, 40, 142, 150–1
eight mundane concerns 134–9, 250
empathetic loving-kindness 181–3
emptiness 53, 210–16, 250
  and interdependence 230–5
enlightenment 56, 250
equalising and exchanging self for others 161, 192–9, 251
equanimity 162
  developing 166–7, 174–81
five Buddhist paths 49
  accumulation 52, 67–8
  meditation 69
  no-more-learning (see *buddhahood*) 69
  preparation 55, 66–7
  seeing 67–9
Gelug 78, 90, 251
Geshe Langri Thangpa
  Eight Verses on Training the Mind 236
great compassion 51, 58, 161, 164–5
Hinayana Buddhism 252
ignorance 19, 202
inherent existence 227, 252
interdependence 6, 8, 206–9
Kadam 86
Kagyu 84, 253
karma 8, 140–2, 253
Karmapa Lama, His Holiness the 84
karmic seeds 32, 145–7
lam rim (or 'stages of the path') 78, 253
liberation 109, 118, 148–9
Mahayana Buddhism (also 'Great Vehicle') 11, 63, 196, 254–5
  difference with Hinayana Buddhism 197

Maitreya 246, 255, 260
  Five Dharmas of Maitreya 246, 255, 260, 263
  The Ornament of Clear Realisation 246
  Sublime Continuum 36, 45, 246, 260, 263
Manjushri 83, 255
Mantra 80–2, 255
meditation 49
  analytical 188, 245
  calm abiding 54, 248
  insight 54, 252
mental events 23–5
  discrimination 28–31
  intention 31–3
  positive 47–8
  temporality of 59–60
Middle Way Consequence school 232, 256
  and correct view 221
Milarepa 256
mind 16, 221–2
  and mental events 26–8
  guarding 58–9
  healing 21–3
  relative nature 43–4
  ultimate nature 44–9
mind of enlightenment (see *bodhicitta*)
Nagarjuna 19, 53, 256, 257, 263
  A Letter to a Friend 134–5
  The Fundamental Wisdom of the Middle Way 248, 257, 264
  The Perfection of Wisdom Sutras 84, 256, 257
  The Precious Garland 263
nirvana 257
Nyingma 85, 257
ocean of samsara 116, 150
precious human rebirth 124–7
refuge 61–2, 258
relationships 173–4, 175–81
renunciation 49–51, 100
  and mind of enlightenment 107
rupakaya 71
Sakya 84, 259
samsara (see *cyclic existence*)

samsaric pleasures 112–14, 150–3
Sangha 89
self, misapprehension of 19–20, 41, 66–7, 214–20
self-cherishing 192–9
selflessness 220–5
sevenfold instruction on causes and effect 161, 181–99, 259
Shakyamuni Buddha 247
  and teaching emptiness 225
  Four Noble Truths 251
  on the nature of mind 24
  on subduing the mind 82
  Sutra on the Ten Grounds 62, 263
  teaching's encapsulated 241
  the Conqueror 105, 107–8
Shantideva 59
six perfections 61, 260
suffering 171
  causes for 143
Tantra (see *Mantra*)
Tsongkhapa, Lama 261
  and Atisha 86–7
  and dependent arising 220
  and Ganden Monastery 89, 250
  and intention 241
  and interdependence 206
  and precious human rebirth 134
  and renunciation 158
  and seclusion 235–6
  In Praise of Dependent Arising 85–6, 220, 263
  life of 83–90
  The Three Principal Aspects of the Path 72, 74, 94–7
  The Great Stages of Mantra 86–8
  The Great Treatise on the Stages of the Path to Enlightenment (also 'Lam Rim Chenmo') 86–8, 90–1, 254
Two Truths, the 226–32, 256, 261
Vasubandhu 21, 245, 261
  Distinguishing the Middle from the Extremes 261
  The Ornament of Sutra 261
  Treasury of the Abhidharma 245, 261
Vinaya 80–2, 262